Ancestral Fi
English Magic

Rebsie Fairholm

articles from Lyra ~
the journal of the Gareth Knight Group

SKYLIGHT
PRESS

© Rebsie Fairholm 2024

First published in Great Britain in 2024 by Skylight Press,
210 Brooklyn Road, Cheltenham, Glos GL51 8EA

The articles in this collection were privately published in *Lyra*, the in-house
journal of the Gareth Knight Group, between 2013 and 2020.

No artificial intelligence tools have been used in the writing, editing, layout or
proofing of this book, nor in the creation of the artwork.

Designed and typeset by Rebsie Fairholm

www.skylightpress.co.uk

British Library Cataloguing in Publication Data:
A catalogue record for this book is available from the British Library.

ISBN 978-1-908011-69-5

Front cover drawing by Rebsie Fairholm based on the Cottingley fairy photos

for
Jim Sparkes
who made me do it

About the Gareth Knight Group

The Gareth Knight Group is a fully contacted working group in the Western Mystery Tradition, serving the folk soul of Britain, working with a group of Inner Plane Adepti or 'contacts,' and guided by them in building bridges between the spiritual worlds and material creation.

The group was founded by Gareth Knight in April 1973, and reached its 50th anniversary in 2023. It meets five times a year in Stroud, Gloucestershire to perform magical workings and meditations, most of which are written by members. The group is currently led by Rebsie Fairholm, Gareth Knight's daughter, who worked alongside him for many years and has been running the group since 2013.

Established in 2012, LYRA is a quarterly magazine published by the Gareth Knight Group and available exclusively to members, written mostly by members of the group. This book is a collection of Rebsie's articles which were written for LYRA between 2013 and 2020.

The Gareth Knight Group welcomes new members. The ability to attend meetings in person is a requirement of membership.

Please see **www.garethknight.org** for more information.

Contents

Margaret Lumley Brown

A haunted house and
the making of a medium

U NLIKE her colleague Dion Fortune, Margaret Lumley Brown has never become a household name in esoteric circles. Perhaps that's not surprising given the high profile Dion Fortune determinedly carved out for herself and the fantastic legacy of books which she left behind. The contribution of Margaret Lumley Brown was more along the lines of simply getting on with the job, quietly and without fuss, within the confines of the Society of the Inner Light, where she lived on the premises and served as the resident arch-pythoness. Charged with the task of taking over Dion Fortune's mediumistic duties following the latter's sudden premature death in 1946, her extraordinary psychism enabled the Society to maintain its force and function for the next 15 years.

Taking on this role was really a case of being plunged in at the deep end. She had no time to train or prepare for replacing Dion Fortune: she was just sat in a room and left to get on with it. She was approaching the age of 60 and had not really done much work of this nature before. Although her gift turned out to be remarkable, it had been latent for most of her life. But this was a time when the Society of the Inner Light was heavily dependent on trance mediumship to maintain its contact with the inner plane Masters, so the pressure and expectation she faced were immense.

The aplomb with which Margaret slipped into her new role is a beautiful example of how a career in the Mysteries can present itself unexpectedly late in life! But it had its origins in a strange experience she had in her youth, while living in London with her sister Isobel in what turned out to be a disturbed house. A casual experiment in parlour spiritualism triggered a full blown haunting and psychic possession. She previously had had nothing more than an intellectual interest in psychism, and nothing had prepared her for an explosive opening of psychic doors.

**Margaret Lumley Brown with Arthur Chichester, warden
of the Society of the Inner Light, c.1950s**

Family origins

Margaret Lumley Brown was born on 7th December 1886 in the
Rectory at Long Stratton, Norfolk. She was the second daughter
of the rector of St. Mary's church, Henry Brown, and his wife
Sarah. (It's often assumed that Lumley Brown is a double-barrelled
surname. It isn't. Lumley was Margaret's middle name.) Her sister
Isobel Kirkwood Brown was some ten years older, born in the
spring of 1877 in the remote village of Little Ouse which sits on

the border of Norfolk and Cambridgeshire. At the time of Isobel's birth Henry Brown was vicar of the small church of St. John on the Cambridgeshire side of the riverbank. The Browns had no other children.

Henry Brown was himself from an ecclesiastical family, born in 1837 at the Rectory in Isham, Northamptonshire, the second of three surviving sons of James Mellor Brown, rector of Isham. James had been born in the British Colonies in Jamaica, where he was a slave-owner, although he did free them before returning permanently to Britain in the 1820s.

In the year following Henry's birth, James Mellor Brown published a pamphlet called *Reflections on Geology* in which he complained about the dangers of science. Scientific philosophy, he warned, was setting people on a path to scepticism, which would eventually lead to loss of faith in the 'absolute truth' of scripture. (Well, time has shown that he wasn't wrong there!)

The newly emerging science of geology was the hot topic of the day and had been upsetting the ecclesiastical applecart by suggesting that the Earth was actually about 600,000 years old, rather than the 6,000 which had always been assumed from a literal interpretation of Genesis. James Mellor Brown objected not only to the conclusions of geology but also to the attempts of other clergymen to reconcile the new science with the Christian faith through theological compromise, believing such clergy to be the well-meaning but unwitting channels for the forces of Satan. He argued hard against the notion of an older Earth, suggesting that the processes of rock formation may have been purposely sped up by God, allowing it to be accomplished in a much shorter time – likening this to the way the journey time from London to Birmingham had been reduced by the invention of the steam engine. Evidence of a protracted ice age could similarly be explained away, since an all-powerful God may have taken it upon himself to rapidly refrigerate the Earth and then quickly thaw it out again. As for the reasons why God might do this, he cautioned that it should not be speculated. After all, it was "dangerous and disreputable to pry into that which has been shrouded from us by Higher Power... surely a humble mind will be ready to confess that events which took place before the birth of man, or the date of revelation, belong to a forbidden province."

As quaint as his position may appear today, such views were held by many people at the time, and to his credit he tried to present a carefully argued case and wasn't simply coming from a perspective of entrenched bigotry. It's perhaps because of this intellectual rigour that his pamphlet is held in high regard by Creationists and evangelical Christians to this day, some of whom are still trying to propagate his ideas.

With such an outspoken clergyman as a grandfather, it's not surprising that Margaret Lumley Brown chose to adopt an assumed name when she began to write about her own forays into "forbidden provinces". In fact, she was descended from a long line of clergymen on her mother's side too.

Her mother Sarah, born in 1848, was among the eldest of fourteen children of the Rev. Edward Thornton Codd, perpetual curate of Cotes Heath in Staffordshire. Sarah's mother was herself the daughter of a clergyman, the Rev. Daniel Copsey of Braintree, Essex – coincidentally also the long time home of Gareth Knight. It was in this small town of Braintree that Margaret Lumley Brown came to live briefly towards the end of her life, though whether she was aware of her own ancestral connections to the town is unclear.

Daniel Copsey was a prolific author of theology books, but died young, and his widow remarried to James Challis, a former pupil of Copsey's charity school, who had spectacularly risen to become Plumian Professor of Astronomy at Cambridge. Thus Margaret Lumley Brown's grandmother grew up living inside the Cambridge Observatory, the magnificent Doric porticoed building which now houses the University's astronomy library but which was then a renowned observatory at the forefront of scientific research and endeavour.

James Challis was a genial, spiritual man who wrote books both about scriptural doctrine and mathematical physics, but is best remembered today for his accidental non-discovery of the planet Neptune in 1846. Despite his tireless search to be the first to find this elusive planet he observed it twice but failed to recognise it, only realising his oversight when another astronomer in Germany had beaten him to it.

All the available indications suggest that the Browns were not an especially close family, and Margaret's relationship with her parents (especially her father) seems to have been decidedly detached. As was the norm for clergymen of the time, they lived a somewhat peripatetic life across much of southern England as Henry Brown was assigned from one parish to another.

Both girls were variously sent off to boarding school or farmed out with relatives, but despite their age gap and the lack of time spent together at home they became very close companions. Isobel was gifted with an exceptional musical talent, and found her natural mode of expression through the piano, while Margaret was drawn more towards writing, especially poetry. Margaret was only 12 when their father died in 1899, and the family had no money left, managing only on a small annuity.

A year later Isobel got married and went to live in Leipzig, where her husband Philip Capel-Dunn was a consular clerk. The marriage was a mismatch, and she soon found herself completely at odds with her husband. At that time marital break-up was a rare event, but nevertheless by 1910 Isobel was back in England without her husband, and her two young children were sent to live with the (now widowed) Sarah Brown. Isobel's situation prompted the two sisters to set up home together for mutual moral and financial support. As it turned out, it was an arrangement which was to see them through the next 27 years.

The 1911 census gives a fascinating snapshot of their lives at this time. They were living at 10 Southwold Mansions in London, part of a block (built c.1901) of red-brick flats in Widley Road, Maida Vale, which still survives today. On the census return, which is written in Isobel's handwriting, Isobel is described as a 33-year-old pianist while Margaret is aged 23 and living on "private means". Every detail given in the census tallies with the situations and events described in Margaret's autobiographical novella *Both Sides of the Door*, and gives us a glimpse into their world in the months immediately preceding their move to a disturbed house and a devastating haunting event.

A Psychic Upheaval

The incident took place in January 1913 when Margaret was 26, and lasted for three weeks. It was a time of great personal trauma for both sisters. Aside from Isobel's marriage break-up, Margaret had lost her fiancé in a street accident. Penniless but independent, the sisters rented a maisonette in a run-down area behind the Edgware Road, close to Marble Arch and to the former site of the Tyburn gallows. Although the exact address is not given in any of her writings, I believe it to have been on the east side of Portsea Place in what was then a terrace of early 19th century townhouses.

From the moment they moved in, the house had an exceptional fustiness which they hadn't been able to shift with any amount of cleaning or fresh air. All the members of the household, which included two female lodgers, began to have regular dreams in which they saw the area as it had been a century earlier, with fields, cobblestones, a brook and a scruffy turnpike. The dreams were remarkably consistent between the four residents.

Things really kicked off however when they decided to have a go at table-turning. The first contact claimed to be Margaret's deceased fiancé, though she didn't believe it was really him. She then tried her hand at automatic writing and found herself channelling a large amount of material from a contact she called Charon – who she later identified more specifically as Oscar Wilde. "As to whether or not it was really he," she later wrote, "I can only say it appeared to all of us to be so at the time."

The presence of other, less benevolent contacts began to crowd in with increasing intensity. One day while out walking in the neighbourhood, Margaret was overcome by a sudden blankness which completely disorientated her. She got lost and couldn't remember who she was or where she was going. Ghoulish figures crouched on benches as she passed and sinister dogs followed her. She found her way home by focusing all her attention on the guiding voice of Charon/Oscar Wilde, and finally made it back to the junction of Edgware Road where "a mass of tangible blackness loomed", enveloping the ghoulish shapes. Her house, when she entered it, looked completely different.

This was the beginning of a three-week period of psychic obsession in which she clung on to her sanity only with the reassurance and support of the Oscar Wilde contact. Unable to sleep for days on end, she found herself opening up as a channel for poetry, which she had dabbled in before but had never been able to produce so spontaneously. She began to pour them out, new poems and remembered ones, for hours at a time. "Words, as such, lost their meaning, but metrical sound acquired an uncanny potency. ...

Each verse appeared in shape before the words grew into it. Thus, a sonnet seemed a square block like a corner-stone, till it undulated gently at the sestet. A villanelle was a delicate elongated box with one end turned back, as it were, to form a much smaller box of the same kind. A ballad was something like the Greek key-pattern. A line said wrongly broke this shape and became an agony."

The fallout was by no means confined to Margaret's illness. The house itself was now subject to a full-blown haunting, witnessed by all the occupants. As Margaret later described it: "At this time the whole house streamed with some kind of electricity. It was a cold January, but the heat, even of fireless rooms, was insupportable. Everything any of us touched seemed electrified. A skin rug rose on end, apparently of itself, before my sister and friend. A dressing gown stood up as though inflated by a form within it, and when touched, sank with a faint whirr to the floor. There must have been some vitalising element also in the air, for flowers fallen behind a chest of drawers in my room were found, more than a week later, still perfectly fresh. Discs of light as large as soup plates spun across the ceiling every night, some of them remaining there, while others spread themselves over us as we lay in bed."

Most unsettling of all was the presence of unpleasant beings which manifested to visible appearance: "They were constantly materialising in front of us, all in medievally demonic shapes. The one most seen had a particularly vile appearance, intensified by a band of fire round its middle. Kitchen utensils and other articles disappeared for days and then were found in unaccountable places. The remarkable fustiness of the house was increased a hundredfold."

One night Isobel was attacked by something which sprang onto her bed. She managed to push it with a thud onto the floor and reach for the light switch, only to find there was nothing there but a deep indentation of its form on the other side of the bed. On another occasion Margaret's room was invaded by a gang of drunken sailors and partially undressed women, who brought with them a strong smell of opium. The women used foul language and said the house was theirs.

At her wits' end and having no experience of dealing with any of these things, Isobel sought help which came in the form of a high profile figure in the Theosophical Society, Robert King. As a Bishop in the Liberal Catholic Church and an accomplished clairvoyant, he was well qualified to give his own impressions and advice. He considered that the house was on the site of a much older building whose conditions still permeated it, and which had hosted all manner of unpleasant activity from opium-taking and prostitution to murder. Consequently it was full of entities who were feeding off the awful psychic atmosphere. His view of Margaret was that she had rare psychic qualities which made her exceptionally vulnerable, and advised that she should go and stay with friends until the atmosphere of the house calmed down – which she did.

The haunting came to an end partly through having run its natural course and partly through the intervention of others. "The elementals, dispersed by the help of a Theosophical lady who kindly offered to come to our assistance, appeared to leave, one by one, through the roof." The only manifestations which remained after this were the discs of light, which still appeared on the ceiling each night but gave the impression of being protective. The sisters continued to live in the house for the next five years without any repeat of the haunting, and the fustiness was also cleared.

After recovering from her ordeal, Margaret wrote up her experiences in vivid detail in her novella, *Both Sides of the Door*. It was published in London at the end of 1918 by Arthur H. Stockwell, a popular vanity publisher of the day, under the pen-name of Irene Hay. Wartime paper shortages meant that the book was printed on poor quality stock, and copies of this original edition are now incredibly rare. It was critically well received though, and was still being discussed in occult magazines in 1923. She evidently sent a copy to Sir Arthur Conan Doyle, who wrote back with great enthusiasm: "It is a unique experience so far as I know. I have been at this subject 30 years and have struck nothing of the kind." He suggested that he would like to meet Margaret and Isobel to discuss it further, and there are follow-up letters indicating that they met with him at least a couple of times.

In 1919 she followed up with a book of poems, *The Litany of the Sun*, which was also well received. After this she appears not to have published any more books, her later writings being non-fiction and mostly in the form of articles and magical diaries. She does seem to have made a systematic effort to develop her psychic faculties in the years immediately following the haunting incident, as evidenced by a notebook she kept around 1916-19 in which she

**A page from Margaret's psychic notebook for
1919, showing encounters with fire elementals**

recorded visual impressions of elementals and planetary spirits she
encountered during her meditations. Other than these startling
sketches, there's little to suggest whether or not she was actively
following a magical path until her arrival at the Inner Light many
years later.

Margaret Lumley Brown lived a colourful life and a free one;
having been put off marriage by the stultifying example set by her
parents and the unhappy adventures of Isobel, she remained single
all her life and fiercely independent. However, a major blow came
in 1937 with the death of Isobel at the age of 59, leaving Margaret
without her closest support and companion.

But it was not long after this that she found her life's vocation, landing herself at the door of the Society of the Inner Light where she met and worked with Dion Fortune, and following the latter's death, moved in at 3 Queensborough Terrace to take up the job of arch-pythoness. And there she remained until her eighties, when a change in the policies and personnel at the Society forced her out, and she was obliged to prevail on the goodwill of relatives.

Isobel's son Denis Capel-Dunn had become a barrister and later a noted military bureaucrat in charge of intelligence operations during World War Two. He was widely tipped for greatness as a political leader, but his career was brought to a premature end in 1945 when the aeroplane in which he was travelling disappeared 300 miles out to sea. His unfortunate legacy is to have been satirised as a pompous character in a series of novels by Anthony Powell. The author had served under him and didn't like him very much, to say the least. Nevertheless, it was Denis Capel-Dunn's widow who took Margaret in when she became homeless in 1972, and I remember as a child being taken to visit them at their beautiful house just outside Braintree.

The fact that I ever met Margaret at all was an extraordinary synchronicity which I remember vividly. It was 1974 and I was walking along the High Street in Braintree with my mum Roma, crossing the cobblestone pavement which once led to the yard of a former coaching inn called The Horn. I was only 5 at the time and I remember having to sidestep to overtake an old lady who stopped suddenly in front of us. As I skipped past her the old lady collapsed and my mum caught her in her arms. After sitting her down on some nearby steps with the help of other passers by (she wasn't seriously unwell and it was just a momentary faint) Roma was astonished to find it was Margaret Lumley Brown, who she recognised from having met her in London more than a decade previously. We didn't know she was living in Braintree, nor that, whether known to her or not, the ancient cobbles on which she collapsed would once have been trodden by her ancestors, being just a couple of hundred yards from the house (now demolished) where her great-grandparents had lived. In fact, my primary school backed onto what was once their garden.

I remember Margaret as a very old-fashioned old lady, all but buried in a huge dark fur coat with a large paste-jewellery brooch, and a voluminous hat which came down over her eyes (the only known photos of her show her much the same way). Other than this I can't claim to have really known her, because although we visited her a couple of times at the Capel-Dunns' house, I was a small child and she never really engaged with me. Years later I was told by her great-niece, Alice, that she didn't really like children very much, which Alice partly attributes to an occasion when she and her siblings were taken to London as children to have tea with Margaret in a posh hotel. After one of Alice's sisters emptied the bowl of sugarlumps into her handbag for her pony, and her brother crawled under the table and bit Margaret's leg, Margaret declined to see them again until they were adults.

Margaret eventually had to move out due to Mrs Capel-Dunn's declining health, and died in London on 27th November 1975 following a minor stroke, little more than a week away from her 89th birthday.

London origins: the spirit of place

I was blown away when I first read *Both Sides of the Door* in my 20s, and was intrigued to try to trace its original location, given that the hauntings were supposedly related to 'place memories' of what had happened there in the past. The strange dreams which Margaret and others repeatedly had in the period immediately preceding the haunting were of a past rural scene in what is now central London. How accurate were those dreams? Slightly at odds with this image of rural idyll, the psychism of Robert King suggested that a house of ill-repute had once occupied the site. Could that be true?

The novella identifies its setting only as the vicinity of Marble Arch, and near the site of the famous Tyburn gallows. After much cross-referencing of maps, descriptions, and nuggets of revelation in Margaret's later writings, I'm reasonably confident that the street in question was Portsea Place, specifically the east side, although identifying the exact house is not such an easy prospect.

In *Both Sides of the Door* Margaret describes the dreams: "There was a stream at the back of this house where some women were washing clothes. The houses round looked quite different, and there were a lot of trees in the distance almost as if it were the country. There was no pavement anywhere, but I saw cobble-stones where

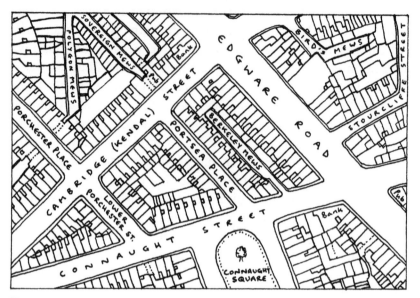

Portsea Place as it was in 1913 when Margaret lived there

Connaught Square is now … There were no yards at the back of the houses as there are now, and the Bayswater Road looked like a country one with trees and cottages rather sparsely scattered over it." An ill-kept turnpike was also a consistent feature in the dreams.

As unlikely a description as that may seem of the area which is now a seething traffic junction, you don't have to go far back in time to reach a point when it was pretty much exactly as described. The lower Paddington area was laid out from the 1820s onward under the possibly tasteless name of Tyburnia, less than a century before the events of the book. Prior to that, it was open fields. The turnpiked Edgware Road marked what was then the westernmost edge of the city, and "Paddington Fields" were still in use as farmland, lightly occupied by cottages, and punctuated by the meandering lines of small streams. An architect's plan of 1824 shows a little bit of building work in progress on the west side of Edgware Road, including the partially completed Connaught Square, but all of the area beyond this was nothing more than the speculative pencil lines of the architect's fancy, boldly rulered across the untouched landscape.

Tyburn was originally a small village, named after the Tyburn stream which ran through it on its way towards the Thames. In medieval times the stream provided London's first piped water supply, and along its banks women washed clothes.

Over time it became polluted by excessive use and abuse, and became a rank, stinking, open sewer. Like most of London's small rivers it ended up buried. Culverted and built over for its entire length, it remains a sewer to this day – its course incorporated into Bazalgette's mighty network of sludge-filled tunnels.

The significance of the Tyburn area goes back much further than the gallows: the site where the Marble Arch stands was previously occupied by Oswulf's Stone, an ancient standing stone which survived until 1869. A map dated 1746 shows a mark close to the gallows which probably represents the stone and charmingly labels it 'Where soldiers are shot'. What happened to Oswulf's Stone nobody knows: it vanished.

Rural Paddington was once a picturesque area beloved by painters, comprising mostly grassland which was cut for hay to feed the city's dairy cattle. The census in 1801 reported little more than 300 cottages across the whole of Paddington. The development of the area began in about 1800, and initially kicked off as a vile and disreputable shantytown. As pressure for housing in the city mounted, a sprawl of wooden shacks for labourers sprang up on the west side of the Edgware Road, often built with a 4 or 5 year land-lease and expected to fall down within that space of time or be subject to swift demolition orders. Within a few years it had become an informal settlement called Tomlins Town, and was so rough and squalid that a ban was made on the leasing of any more building land. This, however, made the problem worse, as the crowding of the existing plots simply became more dense. Between 1811 and 1812 the population of the shantytown almost doubled in twelve months, and the district "had acquired an evil reputation". While it may not be possible to verify whether Margaret Lumley Brown's house was built on the site of this unhappy settlement, the psychic impressions of Robert King are certainly compatible with the historical reality.

In his book *London: The Biography*, Peter Ackroyd relates that when Connaught Square was under construction "a 'low house' on the corner was demolished and quantities of human bodies were found ... other remains were discovered when the neighbouring streets and squares were laid out". For all its later 19th century gentrification, this area was once a grim place.

The 1820s saw a concerted effort to clear up the area and the poor were shunted out. Grand plans for the Tyburnia estate wiped away the makeshift hovels and replaced them with meticulously laid out squares and terraces. Aristocrats and wealthy merchants moved in and the area soon reached a peak of lavishness. Some streets contained more modest homes for tradespeople, and Portsea Place, originally named Upper Frederick Street, was among these. It also quickly became a centre for another kind of trade; nine households in Portsea Place were prosecuted in a crackdown on brothels in 1843.

Margaret's haunted house no longer exists. The whole of the east side of Portsea Place was demolished in 1938 and replaced with a brutalist block of flats called Connaught Mansions, now renamed Portsea Hall. Indeed this large, squat and grimly modern stack erased the entire block of houses between Portsea Place and the Edgware Road along with all their yards and alleys and mews cottages, so it's now impossible to visualise it as it was in Margaret's day. The surviving west side of Portsea Place is a terrace of modest Regency townhouses built from dark grey London brick. The housing on the demolished east side may well have been similar, and gives us one of the only clues as to what kind of building the haunted maisonette might have been.

It may be an expensive area today, but in 1913 the area was deteriorating and unfashionable, a last refuge for well-to-do young ladies down on their luck and unable to afford anything better. Most of the houses had become cheap lodging houses occupied by the dispossessed and down-at heel, backing onto cobbled mews streets running with horse pee where lived the servants and stablehands of wealthier neighbours.

In her later writings, Margaret Lumley Brown gives her own succinct postscript to her 1913 experiences: "Looking back on the events from a distance of some years, they even seem funny sometimes, so much does time alter perspective. Only persons who have been through the same mill will quite understand the awful reality of those three weeks of terror. To most others I quite realise that the whole thing will appear a delusion."

Sources:
Margaret Lumley Brown (Irene Hay), *Both Sides of the Door* (Arthur Stockwell, 1918; Skylight Press, 2011)
Gareth Knight, *Pythoness* (Sun Chalice, 2000)
Various parish records, census records, maps and personal communications.

Originally published in Lyra 13, Samhain 2013

The Wandlebury Goddess

DURING my teenage years when I was thrashing out a spiritual path for myself, largely on the basis of random intuitions, I found a favourite haunt in the circular haven of Wandlebury Ring, a hillfort in the distinctly unhilly landscape of Cambridgeshire. Maintained as a country park, and within cycling distance of the city of Cambridge, it was always busy and full of visitors. It was also well over an hour's drive away from where I lived, so hardly a place for casual visits, and yet I found myself drawn back there again and again. Central to this pull was a powerful goddess contact, which made itself clear to a number of people.

One of the people who seems to have 'met' the Wandlebury goddess, consciously or otherwise, was the archaeologist-dowser T.C. Lethbridge. His disputed discovery of a series of hillfigures at the site in the 1950s caused a major rumpus in academia which eventually saw him marginalised and exiled, and the face of the goddess which he uncovered from the chalk is now reclaimed by grass and brambles. And yet something definitively remains.

As a hillfort, Wandlebury Ring is hardly a great elevated outpost. It occupies the genteel chalky slopes of Gog Magog Hill, rising only to a couple of hundred feet above sea level. But hillforts were not necessarily built for military defence; many were probably communities or ritual sites with a bit of protective ditching to fend off casual intruders, and the available evidence suggests that Wandlebury has never been subject to any violent invasion. Its greatest threat came from King James II who built racing stables and a hunting lodge in the middle of the enclosure. The earthworks are the remains of an Iron Age fort but it's now thought to have been around since the Bronze Age. It once comprised a double circular ditch, but the inner one was shamefully levelled by Lord Godolphin, owner of the house in the 18th century, who simply flattened out the 3,000-year-old earthworks when he wanted to expand his property. His great house is now demolished, although its grandiose stables are still there. Sadly though the earthworks are lost forever, and only the outer ring survives.

T.C. Lethbridge was honorary keeper of Anglo-Saxon Antiquities at a Cambridge museum, and in this capacity he was involved with a 1955 archaeological study of the ring ditch. He soon found himself distracted by his own project focusing on an area further down the slope, just south of the hillfort. Intrigued by legends of hillfigures in the area, which had been described by antiquarians in the 17th and 18th centuries and backed up by local oral folklore and hearsay, he was convinced that the Gog Magog hills had once borne the outlines of an ancient chalk figure of a giant, similar in age and style to the Cerne Abbas giant, and that this had become overgrown and lost to sight by the 19th century. Piecing together all the anecdotes, he became convinced that the southern slope at Wandlebury was the exact location. Being a respected figure in Cambridge archaeology at that time, he managed to get permission to investigate.

Lethbridge's study was controversial from the start. Instead of conventional methods of digging, he used a steel sounding bar to probe the topsoil – a rough-and-ready means of gauging the location of hidden soil disturbances (in the days before the magnetometer was invented). It only works in certain geological conditions, such as those of Cambridgeshire where the local 'clunch' (a chalky rock) is hard and solid when undisturbed but breaks up and turns to mush when exposed to the elements for any length of time. Thus Lethbridge reasoned that if he could push the steel bar into the soil to a greater depth than the natural clunch bedrock, he must in fact be pushing into a man-made hollow in which the clunch had previously been exposed and weathered away. By marking out the edges of such hollows with sticks (artichoke stalks, in fact), a series of lines soon began to emerge on the hillside. But although the sounding bar method had been used successfully by farmers and sextons for years to locate hidden ditches and forgotten graves, it didn't cut much ice with the archaeological establishment, and his efforts met with a frosty scepticism.

But a hillfigure duly emerged, and even Lethbridge was surprised by the results. The anecdotal evidence had all pointed towards the figure of a male giant, widely identified as Gogmagog. So he was a bit taken aback to find that the goggly-eyed bulbous figure in the turf was in fact female.

The further he probed, the more the hillside revealed. After a year and a half he had no less than three figures: a goddess riding a horse, flanked by a warrior wielding a sword and, on the other side, another male figure which Lethbridge interpreted as a winged sun god. Additionally there was a chariot attached to the back of the horse, and a huge crescent moon above the goddess's head.

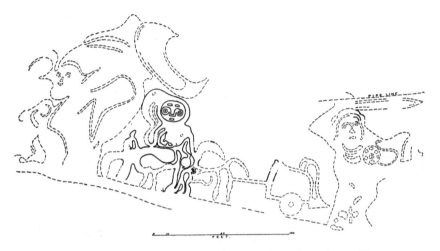

The full range of Wandlebury figures. Dotted lines show the outlines plotted with the sounding bar; solid lines show the parts which were actually excavated. From *Gogmagog: the Buried Gods*, **1957.**

Unfortunately, the archaeology fraternity was not convinced. And you can see their point. Most of the figures wouldn't look like figures at all if they didn't have faces on them, and the left hand one in particular looks like a random collection of squiggles with a smiley face drawn on. You thought the Uffington White Horse was a weird shape? It's nothing compared to this bizarre front-heavy and bobble-headed steed whose enormous beaked face and claw-like snout is far bigger than its stumpy legs. The crescent moon looks more like a dolphin doing a backflip, and it's hard to fathom what made Lethbridge see the left-hand shape as a sun god. While Iron Age art can be idiosyncratic and strangely stylised, it has a rationale and grace to it; these figures simply look like the work of a people who couldn't draw. The only part which looks to have a claim to authenticity, and some resemblance to established 'Celtic' art, is the top half of the goddess.

Lethbridge continued his investigations against a background of increasing doubt and scorn. Some colleagues supported him, others grew concerned that his interpretations were becoming untenable.

Experts were brought in to assess the site and concluded that the lines of the figures were natural, made by an ice-age geological process called solifluction. Lethbridge would occasionally turn up at the site to find that his marker sticks had been pulled up by vandals. Scepticism escalated into open hostility, not helped by the fact that Lethbridge tried to bypass the academic dissent by promoting his discovery in national newspapers and in a book, *Gogmagog: the Buried Gods*. This only served to inflame relations further, including with the owners of Wandlebury who felt it was discourteous, and a disheartened Lethbridge ended up packing in his job and moving down to Devon, where he spent the rest of his life pioneering pendulum dowsing.

By the time the work ended, only a small area representing the head and torso of the goddess had been properly excavated; most of the rest of the figures lie undisturbed under the turf. For a while the goddess remained emblazoned on the hillside in white chalk outlines, making a striking sight from the air. But it was soon decided that the figure should be filled in with turf again, if only for its own protection, and so the goddess once again returned to the earth. At the time I used to visit Wandlebury, in the 1980s, the outlines of her head and face were still visible – though only if you knew where to look.

Over time the opinions of archaeologists have hardened further and Lethbridge's work is widely regarded as erroneous. All the more so since the late 1990s when a further study was carried out at the site using magnetometer and resistivity surveys. These techniques now provide a more accurate method of plotting buried features and past soil disturbance than was possible in the 1950s, and support the view that the outlines are natural geological effects.

But just because the figures are not verifiably real antiquities, that doesn't mean T.C. Lethbridge was wrong! There is a great deal of anecdotal evidence for there having been at least one chalk hillfigure at Wandlebury, but most of the accounts point towards it having been located inside the earthworks rather than on the lower slopes. In which case it would have been definitively erased by Lord Godolphin's 18th century land-flattening spree.

And whatever figures may or may not have been there, it's obvious to anyone with even the slightest sensitivity to inner realities that the presence of a Wandlebury goddess is very real indeed. Her

domain is not within Wandlebury Ring itself but on the very slopes where Lethbridge was compelled to search. Indeed the surviving outlines of Lethbridge's goddess makes a very effective contact point for her. You can sit on the grass between her bulbous eyes and gaze into the woods below, knowing you are in the presence of something profound.

What made the place stand out for me during the 1980s was that everyone in my family made their own spontaneous contact with the Wandlebury goddess, regardless of any differences of magical interests. I'm not sure that ever happened with any other site or contact. I always perceived her to be a benevolent presence, but she's not to be underestimated.

Once when I was sitting on the head of the turf figure I had a very strong sense that the goddess had taken a shine to an amethyst bracelet which my mum had given me for my birthday, and wanted me to donate one of the stones to her. Well I don't mind leaving the odd crystal or bunch of flowers as an offering to a site but there was no way I was going to ruin my lovely bracelet as a sacrifice, so I tried to put it out of my mind. But the impulse kept nagging at me – the goddess wanted one of those amethysts, and was unmoved by my offer to bring her something else next time. It was only when I got into the car to go home that I realised one of the amethysts was missing!

Below the turf figure is a narrow belt of beech trees, screening the site from the busy main road. Everyone in my family agreed that the goddess contact is at its strongest – by far – at the far end of the belt of trees where there stands a large circular mound. This mound is contained within the grounds of the country park but as it's at the far extremity of it, some way south-east of the Ring and down a path that doesn't go anywhere, hardly anyone seemed to go down there and it was usually possible to enjoy some privacy to meditate there even at times when the park was crowded. Standing on top of this tree-covered mound, despite the proximity of the road and the constant roar of traffic, a most extraordinary heightening of the site's power could be felt, so strong it practically made the air tingle. We always wondered if the mound was man-made, and I've since discovered that it is indeed a large tumulus (one of several in the area) which goes by the name of Wormwood Hill. Of course wormwood is a lunar herb sacred to the goddess, but the Victoria County History gives its original name as *Wyrmelawe*, 'the dragon's barrow'. The traditional link between dragons and earth energy scarcely needs to be pointed out. And it seems we aren't the only ones who have singled out this tumulus as a special place of power. Down the parapsychology end of the spectrum you can find reports of whirling bands of coloured light around the mound, audible tones resonating from the earth, spontaneous astral projection, psychic visions of priests in saffron robes and multiple reports of UFO sightings – not to mention those who believe Wormwood Hill is directly involved in the creation of a number of crop circles in the area due to its facility of earth energy accumulation. People interpret their experiences according to their own paths, but many of these experiences are fundamentally not so very different from each other.

The experiences of my mum, Roma, developed into a 'Wandlebury goddess' guided meditation which was used in the Gareth Knight Group at that time and publicly released on an audio cassette recording narrated by Gareth Knight.

Her inner journey began under a great sycamore just above the goddess hillfigure on a summer's evening, facing towards the belt of trees and Wormwood Hill. There are three inner plane female figures to be met in the course of the meditation, but in a sense they are three distinct aspects of the Wandlebury goddess herself. The first is a young auburn-haired woman in a pale green robe, who wears a silver circlet with a green stone in the centre. She is met at the head of the goddess turf figure and initiates the inner plane journey. A second figure, a white-clad woman on a white horse, appears from the belt of trees accompanied by hordes of nature elementals and 'woodfolk'. She represents a faery-oriented aspect of the goddess and becomes the guide for the inner journey. She rides straight at the side of Wormwood Hill which opens up a small gap leading into a stone passageway. The passageway comes out in a cavern in which there are two pools. One is a large circular pool with a mirror-smooth surface. The stone ceiling of the cavern forms into a matching circle directly above it, with a long stalactite in the centre, which slowly drips individual drops of water into the pool, making perfect circular ripples. The woodfolk take great delight in watching their reflections in the pool and seeing them distort into different shapes as the ripples pass outward. The second pool is a stone basin four feet high, shaped like a crescent moon with its horns facing away from the main pool. Between the pools is a high waterfall with three arched bridges going over it. On passing over these three bridges, a dark tunnel of trees is encountered at the back of the cavern – which could be seen as trees growing underground or as the roots of the trees which grow on top of the barrow, and this tunnel leads to the third female figure, seated on a square throne. This silent goddess is the 'seat of power' of the Wandlebury goddess; she wears dark robes with a garland of flowers on her head. For those who want to look, she offers a crystal sphere to gaze into. After making this deepest goddess contact, the journey is retraced to the cavern with the pools. Here the white-clad lady offers a ride on her white horse, which goes galloping out of the hillside and takes the seeker on a wild ride all over the surrounding countryside under the starlight, before eventually depositing them where they started, under the sycamore at the head of the turf figure.

The Wandlebury goddess is not herself a faery contact (as far as I can tell), but she does seem to have some purpose to serve in bridging the gap between human and faery and more specifically in the unification of "man, beast and forest" (otherwise known as the Threefold Alliance). Her aspect as the white lady on the white horse, who gathers and leads the local faery beings, is an example of this, while her green-clad aspect seems more aligned with the human world, and her dark 'within-the-hill' aspect relates to a deeper ancestral and geomagnetic contact. This latter contact has appeared to me in the form of a woman in dark steely-blue robes sitting on a stone seat on top of the mound, eyes closed in stillness, but silently alert rather than asleep, whose dark hair is plaited and tumbles over her robes and twines into the tree-roots, so that you can't tell what is a part of her and what is a part of the trees. The Wandlebury goddess is a complex contact and certainly seems to be something more than a *genius loci*, despite her attachment to this one particular place.

Wandlebury Ring also has its own faery legend, in the form of a fearsome guardian knight. According to a story related by Gervase of Tilbury in the early 13th century, this great knight is supposed to appear to anyone brave enough to challenge him alone by moonlight with the words "Knight to knight, come forth!" Only one person had ever been successful in this, a young knight called Osbert FitzHugh, who made the challenge one moonlit night and found himself confronted by an otherworldly knight on a magnificent horse with black mane and tail and black saddle and bridle. Osbert put up such a brave fight he managed to knock the guardian knight off his horse. He then tried to take the horse away as a prize, but the knight threw a spear at him as he made his escape which pierced him in the thigh. At first he didn't notice the injury, and as the knight had disappeared he made his way home with the horse. His possession of it was a short-lived triumph; it broke free and vanished at the break of day. And in the tradition of such encounters, the wound made by the spear, although ostensibly healed, would bleed afresh every year on the anniversary of the combat.

This legend does clang a few chimes with some other ancient British legends, including of course those of the Grail. The wounding in the thigh with a spear, and the refusal of the wound to fully heal, is well established as the fate of the Fisher King, and variants of it apply to other characters in several of the Grail legends.

Many folklorists have come unstuck with the guardian knight by taking his tale too literally, and trying to interpret the legend at face value as a combat with a physical knight, while others see it as a simple ghost story, but it will be obvious to anyone with esoteric experience that he is a faery guardian. He is summoned at dead of night, the liminal point where one day meets the next, and serves in the role of the classic guardian of a sacred site. His faery horse, when taken into the human world, does not retain any physical form beyond the next 'crossover' point of daybreak. The nature of the annual cyclical wound (inflicted with the spear, a faery weapon) is also typical of faery lore, each anniversary being the crossing-over point where the knight's influence comes back into play. The fact that Osbert initially doesn't feel the thrust of the spear is another indication of its otherworldly nature.

Another Wandlebury legend has it that a golden chariot is buried somewhere on the site. This kind of myth is again quite widespread and is another nugget of faery lore, which commonly links golden objects with faery hills and sidhe mounds (whether they be barrows or natural hills). Again, the tendency to take these myths too literally has resulted in many ancient sites being wrecked by treasure-hunting twits over the years, particularly in the 18th and 19th centuries as materialism became the majority mindset.

Trying to pull together so many different strands of mythology, tradition and psychic experience is a challenge, but when so many interesting things converge at the same site, it does at least highlight something that is worthy of further investigation.

Sources:

T.C. Lethbridge, *Gogmagog: the Buried Gods* (Book Club Associates edition, 1975 – originally published in 1957)

Terry Welbourn, 'The Buried Gods of Gogmagog' in *British Archaeology*, issue 112, May/June 2010.

Originally published in Lyra 14, Imbolc 2014

Wyrd and Wortcunning
Anglo-Saxon Magic Revisited

MY introduction to Anglo-Saxon magic came at a relatively early age, and looking back on it, served as an important part of my apprenticeship to magic in general. Before the 1980s hardly anybody seemed to be aware that there was an Anglo-Saxon magical tradition. Even today, it's rare to come across anyone practising it, as it's heavily eclipsed by the ever-popular Celtic tradition. Part of the reason for that, of course, is that Celtic mythology is exceptionally rich and well preserved and contains enough worthwhile material to keep anyone going for a couple of lifetimes. But the Anglo-Saxon material is also out there. You just have to take a bit more trouble to look for it.

The first time it burst into popular consciousness was when Brian Bates' *The Way of Wyrd* came out in 1983. Written as a novel, it tells its story through the eyes of a Christian scribe who arrives in England to convert the pagan Saxons and ends up being educated, and eventually initiated, by a Saxon sorceror or cunning man. Although presented as fiction it's very much in the spirit of ludibrium, filled with nuggets of Anglo-Saxon magical lore researched from old manuscripts.

The core of it is a fundamental energy called *Wyrd*; at its most basic level a concept of Fate – but a fluid and controllable Fate based on the polarised principles of Fire and Frost. The dynamic interaction between these polarities creates a universal energy of life, a concept not a million miles away from the druidic Awen or the Eastern Chi, but visualised in the form of a great three-dimensional cosmic web which interconnects all things. Each touch upon the Web of Wyrd sets up a resonance which ripples along the threads and affects the whole of Creation.

This provides the explanation for how the magic works, because a small ritual action done with focused intent will set up a resonance with its relevant counterpart along the threads of Wyrd. With this central teaching at its heart, the book presented a treasure trove of spells, charms, ceremonies and healing craft, along with clear practical instructions and an explanation of their inner dynamics. And while some of them fell into the "don't try this at home" category, others were eminently practical.

At this time, my brother and I were both teenage amateur magicians, and the release of this book brought a deep frisson of excitement. We hadn't seen anything like it before, and it really felt to us like a great revelation of secret powers. Obviously there was no shortage of occult books in our house, but we were both instinctively drawn towards paganism and earth magic, and didn't see much appeal in all the tedious Qabalah stuff our parents were into. And in those pre-internet days you were limited to whatever decent books you could snap up in the Mind, Body & Spirit section of your local bookshop, or (excitement of excitements) the occasional trip to the Atlantis Bookshop in London to blow six months' worth of pocket money.

It was my brother who found and bought *The Way of Wyrd* when it came out. I still remember the thrill of being shown this wonderful new book with its practical revelation of the whole shebang of Anglo-Saxon magic, and the prospect of using it to make myself a real magician. Here at last was a direct source of pure occult knowledge, and a much quicker path to adepthood than rummaging through Gareth Knight's bins or building a shrine to the goddess Epona on my windowsill. However, to maintain the balance of filial power, my brother merely dispensed small chunks of wisdom from it on an occasional basis – much as the main character in the book learns his craft from the sorceror. I was sorely tempted to sneak into his room and borrow it secretly while he was out, but I was scared of getting on the wrong side of the Elemental Guardian which he claimed was protecting his bedroom.

One day when we were out walking the dog in the fields near our house, we were disturbed to find that one of the little places we considered to be sacred – a cluster of trees with a wooden bridge going over a tiny stream – had been defiled with litter. We pondered what to do about this. Normal public-spirited teenagers might have gone home and fetched a bin-bag, but for some reason this never crossed our minds. Instead, we decided that the solution was to make a rune-stick. This was a special technique we'd learned from *The Way of Wyrd* which we could use to put a protection on the place. We selected a dry piece of twig from the ground (not cut directly from a tree), and I carefully made the rune-stick under his instruction. First I used my penknife to slice a section of bark off, to provide a flat, whitish panel along one side of the stick. Using my own knowledge of runes, which was quite good at that time, I selected five or six suitable protective symbols, then burned them into the wood using my cheap crappy soldering iron from Argos, which had a few pyrography nibs included with it. The secret, my brother explained, was to empower the runes by focusing very hard on their intended purpose all the while I was inscribing them. This I did. Finally, my brother told me I needed to cut a notch into the top of the stick to provide it with a mouth, so that the stick could talk to the spirits. Without this, the runes wouldn't work. I dutifully carved a notched mouthpiece into the end, and we went back to the besmirched site and placed the stick upright into the soft mud underneath the bridge. When we went back the next day, the litter was all gone. No more litter appeared there during the time the stick was there either. It worked.

Over the next year or two we used rune-sticks on a number of occasions where protection of vulnerable sites was needed, and they never let us down.

These days I rarely have occasion to do this kind of practical magic, or spellcraft as it might be more appropriately called. My brother has moved on completely, happy in his engineering career, and no longer practices magic. But the Saxon connections keep popping up. We grew up in Essex – the land of the East Saxons – but were born beside the Severn in Gloucestershire in what was once the Saxon tribal kingdom of Hwicce, still loaded with Saxon remains. Our mum was born and brought up in the heart of King Alfred's country in Somerset, a fact which came to life very strongly in her own esoteric endeavours.

None of these things are special in themselves; most people have similar connections to their immediate Saxon landscape and ancestors, and once you start looking for them they seem to pop up everywhere. I now live within five miles of Deerhurst, a very significant Saxon ecclesiastical site, and every time I go there I feel the tingles along the web of wyrd which still connects us to the considerable and largely untapped magical tradition of our Saxon forebears.

Wyrd or not, it would be wrong to suggest that there is any cohesive, definable tradition which could be labelled 'Anglo-Saxon magic'. We are talking about a period of several centuries, from around 410 AD to the Norman Conquest of 1066. We're also talking about assorted tribes of Angles, Saxons and Jutes, living in competing kingdoms, each with their distinct cultures, intermingling with the various Celtic cultures which were already established. More drastically, we're talking about the period in British history when Christianity was introduced to these shores, meaning that we have both Christian and pagan traditions, along with whatever spontaneous or strategic intermingling of them may have occurred. And any study of sources is necessarily oblique, because so little survives in the way of original Anglo-Saxon writings and much of what we have comes from medieval 'copies' of lost texts.

As in so many magical explorations, the best way in is through your imagination.

Until recently, the Anglo-Saxon period was commonly referred to as the Dark Ages, named not for their inherent darkness but for our own lack of enlightenment, since so few writings have survived

Anglo-Saxon spiral-carved font in Deerhurst priory church, Gloucestershire. It served for many years as a washtub in a local farmyard before being rescued by a Victorian vicar.

to tell us about it. It's not that the cultural treasures never existed; the Saxons had spectacular libraries at monastery sites such as Lindisfarne and Jarrow (the stunning Lindisfarne Gospels are a surviving sample). They had skilled craftspeople and appreciated beautiful artwork – not dissimilar to Celtic art with its beasties and spirals – which can be seen in the decorative stone carvings in their surviving churches. They adored music and song, and had a great love of harps and lyres, enough of which have survived archaeologically that it's possible to replicate Anglo-Saxon lyres today with some accuracy, even if the tuning info and the music itself has been lost.

The main reason so little has survived from the Saxon era is because of the ferocity and persistence of the invading Danes, who spent some 70 years ranging up and down the country ruthlessly trashing, burning and looting. Consequently we have to make the best of the material we have and find our own path into it.

The most famous surviving work of Old English literature is the epic poem *Beowulf*. At face value it doesn't appear to hold much magical content and is mainly famous as a bloody tale of marauding flesh-chewing monsters and limb-hewing heroes. But there are the bare bones of an initiatory pattern underneath the warrior drama.

The hero Beowulf confronts three separate challenges: first the troll-like Grendel who attacks him within the barred and bolted halls of human dwelling. Then the more nebulous spectre of Grendel's mother, whose realm is the stagnant waters of the mere. And finally he deals with an angry dragon who dwells within a tumulus, guarding a hoard of gold.

In these three locations we can see three clear planes of consciousness: the homely level of normal human consciousness, with the barricaded hall representing the confines of the physical body; the astral or imaginative level represented by the waters of the murky mere, with a female 'monster' to confront; and finally the true Underworld, spiralling down into the Inner earth, and from which the hero cannot return alive.

The description of the dragon's tumulus is a classic entrance to the Underworld: a stone-roofed barrow with a hidden passageway leading deep inside, fronted by a stone arch where a stream gushes forth. It evokes some very familiar visions of the spiralling earth-energy 'dragons' which are still readily discernible at barrows, hills and mounds. Folklore about golden treasure hoards inside barrows persisted well into the last two or three centuries, and many Neolithic barrows have been destroyed by diggers in the mistaken belief that they were stuffed with physical (rather than Otherworldly) gold.

The dragon-in-the-earth motif also resonates with other native British legends, most obviously the *Historia Brittonum* story of Merlin, in which the agitated dragons beneath a pool deep under the earth are responsible for the continual failure of Vortigern's tower. This is explained symbolically as

Early 9th century[?] beastie head at Deerhurst priory church.

the white dragon of the Saxons fighting with the red dragon of the Celts, but there's a power in these images that goes far deeper than simple political allegory. Perhaps we're back to the Saxon *wyrd* again, with its polarised energies of Fire and Frost.

The pagan Anglo-Saxons weren't big on gods. A handful of names spring to mind – Wayland, Woden, Frig and Tiw – but they didn't really go in for pantheons of major named gods like other ancient cultures, and they didn't often build shrines to them. Their focus seems to have been more directly on aspects of Nature, such as Sun, Moon, trees, springs and Mother Earth.

They did revere ancestors and may well have had some localised gods and ancestor deities, but for the most part they found their spirituality in the landscape. Pope Gregory disparagingly described the Saxon religion as "the worship of sticks and stones". Perhaps unsurprisingly, they also had a strong Faery tradition, encompassing the dark dwarves of inner earth and the refulgent elves or Shining Ones.

As well as the potent mythology found in epic poetry, we have some actual recipes for practical magic in two 9th to 10th century manuscripts, the *Lacnunga* and *Bald's Leechbook*. These are actually medical books, but to the Saxons magic was intimately bound up with healing. The practice of Anglo-Saxon medicine was known as leechcraft: nothing to do with bloodsucking invertebrates, it's from the Old English *læce* (doctor) and *cræft* (skill). Healing was an inseparable mix of herbal remedy and ritual magic.

We can still recognise many Saxon healing herbs through the survival of the Old English *wyrt* in the names of plants today, such as mugwort (a digestive stimulant), hedge woundwort (formerly used for staunching and healing wounds) and of course St. John's wort (enjoying a resurgence as a proven antidepressant), and many others.

There is an intriguing Nine Herbs Charm in the *Lacnunga*, interpreted as a remedy for infected wounds. Each of the nine herbs – mugwort, betony(?), lamb's cress, plantain, mayweed, nettle, crab-apple, chervil and fennel – is added to the mix with its own magical incantation.

After adding the first six herbs, the healer sees the spirit of the infection approaching the patient in the form of a serpent. Using nine rune-sticks, carved with the initial letter-rune for each herb, the healer invokes the power of Woden to strike the serpent-spirit into nine pieces:

"A serpent came crawling; it bit someone's flesh. Then Woden took nine glory-twigs; smote the serpent so that it flew into nine parts."

Before applying the herbal salve to the wound, another incantation is sung into the patient's mouth and both ears, and finally over the wound itself.

Another charm in the same book gives a remedy for sudden stabbing pains, which are attributed to an invisible spear or arrow shot by a supernatural adversary. The cure involves removing the 'elf-bolt' with a special magically charged iron knife and sending it back to its originator, the knife afterwards being placed in running water.

Such folk-ritual work is not of much direct practical value to modern magicians – at least not as a substitute for medical care. But in its fundamentals it has validity. The repetition of a charm or incantation with focused intent is not so very different from what we practice in modern ritual magic, and I can't think of any more effective way of neutralising negative energies from an object or magical weapon than placing it in running water. That's exactly what I would do!

But there is something really extraordinary about all this smiting of spirits and removal of faery weapons. And that is that these texts belong to the 9th and 10th centuries, several hundred years *after* Britain had been Christianised.

Some of the charms include appeals to Christ or the Blessed Virgin, but it's clear that the Saxons still made much use of nature spirits and faery lore, and saw no conflict in doing so. Certainly in the late Saxon period there were efforts by the Church to prohibit pagan remedies and witchcraft, but either the prohibition wasn't very effective or the practice of pagan-style magic was more widely used and tolerated than one might assume.

These are not isolated examples either; other texts give full-scale pagan rituals with a wafer thin veneer of Christian piety, including some which must have been practised with the full knowledge and co-operation of the parish priest, such as the remarkable *Æcerbot*, or Field-Remedy, a blatant crop fertility rite, which involved cutting

The door of the Saxon temple. Enter if ye will!

four turfs from a field (one from each quarter) and placing them in church with the grassy side towards the altar, before returning them to the field with herbs, rune-sticks and a bit of invocation to bring the seed of the sun-god to Mother Earth.

So much for my becoming an adept by reading *The Way of Wyrd*. What I really learned is that the Anglo-Saxon tradition is vast and fascinating, and my little rune-sticks barely scraped the surface.

Originally published in Lyra 16, Lughnasadh 2014

Old English Tree Runes
Lore of the Sacred Five

RUNES were in use in this country, in one form or another, from the Bronze Age right up until the end of the Anglo-Saxon period, when they were gradually replaced by the Roman alphabet as Britain became Christianised (not because runes were inherently pagan, but because of cultural changes which favoured Latin as a scholarly language). They served a dual purpose: as an alphabet for written communication, and as an esoteric system of named symbols which could be used for both divination and magic.

There are many variants of the runic alphabets, but they all contain common characters relating to important everyday concepts, objects and natural forces, such as ice, sun, year, gift, joy, horse, water and mouth (to reduce them down to their simplest meanings). There are also some which represent trees. These seem to have been more important to the English than to other rune-using cultures. The standardised Common Germanic Futhark has three runes named after trees, while the English Futhorc alphabet has five.

If you go down to the New Age bling shop today, the rune sets you'll see for sale almost invariably comprise the Common Germanic Futhark, or Elder Futhark. So ubiquitous is this standardised set of 24 characters that many people assume it's the only correct and authentic rune alphabet. In fact there are many others, or – to look at it another way – none at all, because runes evolved over a wide area and a long period of time, and there was no standardisation of the alphabets in the days before printing and mass-literacy. The Elder Futhark itself is merely a scholarly best guess at a standard rune alphabet, based on the scant available source material.

In England, the number of runes expanded from 24 to around 30 to accommodate the developing sounds and spellings of the English language, and among these new additions were two more tree runes. The importance of tree symbolism to the early English is reflected in these extra runes, telling us something about which trees dominated the English landscape and consciousness at that time.

It would be misleading to conflate the tree symbols in runic alphabets with the better known "tree alphabet" of Ogham. Runes include many non-tree symbols; they are also probably not directly related to Ogham. There are no such things as 'Celtic runes'. Iolo Morganwg's 18th century invention of a Welsh Bardic rune alphabet, the Coelbren y Beirdd, may be a workable system in its own right, but ancient Celtic it ain't. Runes specifically and exclusively belonged to the Germanic languages such as early Norse, English, Danish, German and Icelandic. That's not to say, however, that Celtic symbolism should be banished from any study of runes. There are many common threads running through the lore of Celtic, Anglo-Saxon and Norse mythology, so although the runic and Ogham alphabets differ in form, practice and origin, their impulse springs from a common source.

The purpose of the runes goes a lot deeper than the casual divination which accounts for most of their popularity today. As a divination tool they lack the finer detail of the Tarot but nevertheless can be very effective indeed in their own way. Just as the Tarot images contain powerful archetypal principles, so do the runes – albeit somewhat further removed from us in time and culture. Each rune is a self-contained magical gateway, not just for use as a personal oracle but as a means of connecting with the fundamental aspects of the Planetary Being and forces of Nature.

The five trees found in Old English Futhorc runes are oak, ash, thorn, birch and yew. And surely it's no coincidence that the modern English words for all five trees have evolved directly from Old English, in some cases with no change in pronunciation.

āc – oak
sound: **a**

æsc – ash
sound: **æ**

þorn – thorn
sound: **th**

beorċ – birch
sound: **b**

ēoh – yew
sound: **iw**

It would be nice if we could align these five tree rune concepts into a table of correspondences to fit our existing five-fold structures, such as the Four Elements + Spirit which make the basis of our pentagram symbols. But they don't naturally fall into pre-ordained categories, and to shove them into arbitrary Elemental attributions would be to miss out on what they really have to say. They seem not to comply with the pure Elemental forms but are a more nuanced way of expressing planetary forces. This shouldn't really be a surprise, as the Planetary Being and all its generative powers derive from a blend of different elemental forces, in harmony or in tension, and this is how they are expressed through Nature. It's rare to encounter the Elements in their pure form in the natural world. So although the Elements are fundamental components of the forces which these runes represent, they don't always come neatly separated for the convenience of occultists.

So how do we make magical sense of them? The only real solution is to work with them meditatively and see what comes up. To this end, I've provided a gateway image for each rune which should serve as a meaningful starting point. The beauty of the runes is that they're very powerful symbols, tingling with an energy which is ready to be tapped into, so even a modest effort brings results.

We also have some clues from the people who created and used them, although in the time-honoured way, these come in the form of riddles which are not always easy to solve! The main source is an Old English rune poem which survives only in a book from 1705, as the original Saxon manuscript it was taken from is now lost. Its authenticity is not in doubt though, as similar rune poems have survived in Norwegian and Icelandic. The language of the poem suggests it may have originated in south-east England in the 9th century. It provides some insight into what the runes meant to the Anglo-Saxons, though not, alas, in a way which makes obvious sense. The verses are highly cryptic and obscure (all the more so because of ambiguities in translation to modern English) and you have to work at them to get anything out of them.

 āc (pronounced *ahc*). **Oak.** The oak is the quintessentially English tree and has a long association with kingship, sovereignty and masculine energy. Pubs called the Royal Oak still abound as a relic of its kingly status. It's a strong and majestic presence in the landscape and was often planted as a boundary marker in past centuries, so you can still find spectacular ancient specimens at field margins and on village greens all over the country.

As if to reinforce these associations with masculine strength, the oak is sacred to the gods of thunder in several mythologies (Jupiter and Thor) and is particularly prone to being struck by lightning. The main rational reason for this is that the oak tends to be taller than other trees, and therefore the easiest target for lightning. And on the basis that lightning never strikes the same place twice, it was believed until relatively recent times that a piece of wood from a lightning-struck oak would protect whoever carried it or kept it in their house from a lightning strike. The lightning-struck oak is a powerful symbol in its own right, often blasted out at the heart, sometimes with a hollow core large enough for a person to get inside (which is quite an experience!)

In the Icelandic *Völsung Cycle*, the mythical King Völsung builds a great hall with a living oak tree growing in the middle, named the Barnstokkr. During a great feast, the god Odin turns up and thrusts his sword deep into the tree. Only the sword's rightful owner will be able to withdraw it, he claims. Sure enough, none of the guests is able to remove the sword except for Völsung's son Sigmund.

This use of the oak tree and sword to bestow sovereignty has a clear parallel with King Arthur's withdrawal of the sword from the stone.

As a force of nature, this rune represents the fiery forces of the Planetary Being blasting through into manifestation. Such powers may be precise and direct (as in the bestowal of kingship) or they may appear random and oblique, but either way they are directed from elsewhere and are beyond the control of mankind. The image of the lightning flash on the Tree of Life is a good representation of it – raw natural force which comes from a higher power and just does its thing in accordance with divine law.

The rune poem gives us a rather cryptic verse to work with. As the oak rune **āc** is unique to the Anglo-Saxon Futhorc, there is no equivalent verse in the Norwegian or Icelandic rune poems, so we have to puzzle out this version as best we can. It reads:

> *oak is for the sons of men on earth*
> *a feeder of flesh, often travels*
> *over the gannet's bath, the ocean tests*
> *whether the oak keeps good faith*

This may look like gibberish, but 'the gannet's bath' can probably be interpreted as the sea, which the oak travels over in the form of a ship – oak being the favoured wood for ship-building due to its great durability and strength.

The meditative image for this rune is a broad, majestic oak tree standing on the horizon in an open field in late summer; the field is full of golden ripened wheat. Nothing else is visible except the expanse of wheat field and the cloudless blue sky, against which every branch and leaf and twist of the oak tree is clearly defined. As you approach this great presence, its crown seems to coalesce into pointed dark gold shards, as if becoming a living royal crown.

æsc (pronounced *ash*). **Ash.** It's curious that the modern English word 'ash' is pronounced exactly the same as the Anglo-Saxon word **æsc**, even though the spelling has completely changed! The ash tree has a very significant place in Northern European mythology, being the archetypal Yggdrasil, the great cosmic ash tree which unites the 'nine worlds', and whose three main roots reach down into three wells (i.e. three planes of existence), and in whose presence the gods are said to hold court. It has a particular association with the god Odin, who submitted to be hanged from it for nine days and nights in pursuit of wisdom.

Yggdrasil belongs specifically to Norse myth, and while the Anglo-Saxon people had their own version, Irminsul, which is very similar, the Saxon myth has seven worlds rather than nine and the world tree is actually a yew! So we can't assume that the ash tree had such lofty cosmic associations for them as it did for the Vikings. The Saxons revered the god Odin in his Anglicised form, Woden, and not just in pre-Christian times either. Woden remained a vitally important god in England even within Christian society, and his name is still with us in the word 'Wednesday'.

The ash puts in another appearance in Norse myth, as the first human beings, Askr and Embla, were created from trees. Odin and his two brothers breathed a soul into an ash tree which they found on the seashore, and named it Askr (Old Norse for Ash).

On a more everyday level, the ash tree is associated with protection, and particularly protection from snakes. An English folklore tradition has it that anyone wearing or carrying an ash staff will be avoided by adders. More to the point, it's a favoured wood for a magical wand. The witch's stang (a tall forked staff) is traditionally made of ash. It also makes very fine spears and arrows, which is probably the meaning behind the final line in the rune poem for **æsc**:

> *ash is very tall, dear to men*
> *strong in foundation, holds its place properly*
> *though many men fight against it*

Ash wood is strong, dense and flexible and grows long straight poles when coppiced, so it is favoured for making tool-handles and boat oars as well as being the wood of choice for weapons. It burns exceptionally well even when green, and is traditionally used for Yule logs. Because of its density it burns for a long time and generates a lot of heat. Symbolically it is the bright fire of inspiration, piercing down from a higher plane.

If the oak rune represented fiery forces blasting through with all the subtlety of a lightning flash, the ash rune represents the same fiery forces brought under control and set to work for mankind with skill and precision. Focused, directed and straight. The arrow is an apt symbol here.

The magical image to open the portal of **æsc** is a tall, straight-trunked ash tree growing on a grassy plain, at the head of a clear pool in which its image is reflected.

þorn *(pronounced thorn).* **Thorn.** The thorn rune looks very like what it represents, and also has the distinction of having been incorporated in the Romanised alphabet for many centuries; it can be seen in any text written in Old English, in the form of the symbol 'þ' which is based on the original rune (one of two runes to be adopted into the Roman alphabet). It looks a bit like a letter 'p' with the loop dropped half way down the stem, but it represents the sound 'th'. It fell out of usage in the early medieval period, which is a bit of a shame as it actually served quite a useful purpose!

There are of course many different species of thorn tree, but the rune **þorn** is taken in the generic sense, a generalised thorn tree, because its inhospitable spikes are what matters for its symbolic purpose. If it does refer to a specific type of thorn though, the most likely candidate is probably blackthorn, the tree traditionally associated with winter and bitterness, rather than its sister tree hawthorn, which is more associated with May blossoms and spring joys. The rune poem makes clear that the thorn rune is an uncomfortable one.

> *thorn is painfully sharp to any warrior,*
> *it is bad to seize it, excessively severe*
> *for any person who lies with it*

The image we have here is of something which should neither be purposely grasped nor passively dwelt with. Its sharpness cannot be avoided, but it's extremely severe for those who choose to rest upon it or surround themselves with it. In other words, it causes the greatest pain to those who seek it out or wallow in its cruelty. Its sharpness does however serve a very necessary purpose, to prod us out of complacency and needle us into action. As a planetary force, it represents the harsh and uncomfortable forces which keep things moving, and discourage things from becoming settled and stagnant. Thorn is the stimulating rune!

There are many folklore traditions associated with thorn trees, from the legendary 'Eildon Tree' where Thomas the Rhymer was scooped up by the Queen of Faery, to the persistent superstition that it's unlucky to bring May blossom into the house. It has special status in Glastonbury as the tree which blossomed from the staff of Joseph of Arimathea, and notoriety as the Crown of Thorns worn by Christ.

However, it's the dark-skinned and sloe-bearing blackthorn which most closely fits the Anglo-Saxon concept of **þorn**, with its ferocious spiked thorns and tendency to grow into dense thickets. The Saxons seem to have associated it with warriors and the cruelties of battle. It has a protective function too, since its thorns are not to be messed with, and traditionally its wood makes an effective magical wand or staff.

In its protective role it puts in an evocative appearance in the fairy tale of Sleeping Beauty, in which the heroine is imprisoned behind an impenetrable wall of blackthorn. This tale is no Victorian whimsy, but a sweetened version of a very ancient tale, first written down in the 14th century text *Perceforest* but with roots going deep into oral tradition.

While this may not be the most comfortable rune to work with, it shouldn't be feared or avoided. Its magical portal can be built up in the form of a dense tower of twisted and interwoven thorn branches, akin to the hawthorn tower which imprisoned Merlin. It doesn't much matter whether you use the image of hawthorn with its white blossoms and blood-red haws, or blackthorn with its long spikes and dusky black sloes. The principle is to accept a few unavoidable jabs but to keep moving around it and searching its apparently impenetrable façade for a way in. Sooner or later, the entrance will be found.

beorc (pronounced *beyorch*). **Birch.** The delicate shape and pale silvery bark make birch an obvious Faery tree. It has a light, bright, airy aura about it. Its wood is very hard and very strong, but also lightweight, which gives it a lot of practical uses, including the soundboards of musical instruments such as harps, where it produces a beautiful tone while remaining strong and stable (and thus keeping tune). It's another wood traditionally used for the Yule log because it burns exceptionally well, a characteristic which would've meant a lot to our ancestors. But unlike long-lasting ash, birch burns up very quickly.

The birch rune is the expression of the planetary energy of youth and vigour. A breath of fresh air in every sense. It's the energy which puts a spring in our step and keeps our flame of aspiration burning bright. The rune poem casts it as a tree of beauty and grace, and the epitome of youth in that it doesn't go to seed but regenerates itself perpetually by means of fresh green shoots.

> *birch is fruitless, yet bears*
> *shoots without seeds, is pretty in its branches*
> *high in its spread, fair adorned*
> *laden with leaves touching the sky*

I had a particularly clear 'vision' of the meditative portal for **beorc**, which seemed to conjure a scene of early summer. A very lively birch tree grows on top of a grassy mound in warm bright sunlight. Its leaves are a bright yellow-green and its trunk shining white, mottled with grey. A dynamic breeze is blowing around it and setting all its leaves and branches dancing and shimmering. It's an image of life, light and vigour. Within the front of the mound is an opening, lined with large stones – an entrance passageway, though all is dark inside and nothing is visible. A faint, low, flutey sound emanates from the entrance as the breeze blows across it.

ēoh (pronounced *yiw*). **Yew.** The magical associations of the yew tree are deep and ancient. It's familiar to us today in churchyards up and down the country, where some impressively ancient specimens can be found. A little while ago I visited the church of Iffley near Oxford – a Norman church full of wonderful 12th century carvings – which has a spectacular ancient yew tree beside it, and one with quite extraordinary vibes to boot! Only afterwards, when I read that the tree was over 1,500 years old, did it suddenly occur to me that it predated the church by some margin. It would already have been a good 600 years old when the church was built – so the church was sited to be close to the tree, not vice versa. It made me wonder how often this has been the case with other churchyard yews. Some of these trees are so old they would've been around in the time of our Saxon ancestors.

Yews are renowned for their exceptional longevity, and their wood is also very hard and durable. They are not to be trifled with though – all parts of the tree are poisonous, a warning that its power is not to be misused. Yew represents the planetary force of transmutation. If birch brings us change through the bright and breezy dynamic of youth, yew is a static presence which gives us a more fundamental and drastic transformation – an instant transition from one state to another.

The yew tree is the world tree in Saxon mythology, diverging from the Norse ash. It is the tree which connects us to our root ancestors and our far descendants. It links the heaven worlds with the underworlds. It represents an earthly manifestation of the spirit of Creation and a vehicle for the Planetary Being.

As far as the rune symbolism goes, **ēoh** is the boundary between the worlds. It's a place of crossing-over, and a contact point with the oldest of ancestors. Mythologically it is the tree which brings spiritual forces down into the plane of manifestation.

In *The Leaves of Life*, an English folk song which always gives me tingles, it becomes the tree of crucifixion:

> *And there you will find sweet Jesus Christ*
> *With his body nailed to a yew tree*

This may be a reference to the tradition that the cross was made of yew wood, but it feels much deeper than that to me. The image which always comes to me is of a resplendent, risen Christ figure, not a grisly hanging scene. Sometimes the figure on the tree is not Christ, but Woden. The legend has it that he was given the runes after his initiatory ordeal hanging from the world tree.

The rune poem says:

> *yew is an unsmooth tree outside*
> *hard, earthfast, fire's keeper,*
> *underpinned with roots, a joy in the homeland*

The mention of earthfast roots tie in with its status as an ancestral tree, but the reference to fire's keeper is more obscure. One to meditate on, perhaps!

To find the magical portal of the **ēoh** rune, imagine a dark grove of yews in the gloaming. Only small patches of twilight sky are visible under the dense canopy of dark evergreen branches, and the vague shape of a crescent moon behind a veil of cloud. While you can see the coarse bark of a vast ancient yew in front of you, the air seems obscured by a dark green mist. The vast trunk is open and hollow, forming a great crescent. There is a feeling of slight disorientation, and then a momentary flash of starlight down below makes it not quite clear which way up things should be. If, while contemplating this portal, the world is suddenly turned upside-down, then you've found it!

A study of the Anglo-Saxon tree runes would not be complete without stopping to take note of the trees which are *not* included. We don't know whether the five chosen trees were deemed to be special and significant, or whether they just happened to find their way into the line-up. Apple and hazel are obvious candidates which you might expect to see in any British pantheon of sacred trees. Elder, alder, holly and willow are also conspicuous by their absence. Other trees we think of as quintessentially English such as beech, elm and sycamore were probably not included because they may not have figured very strongly in the Anglo-Saxon landscape in the way they have done in more recent times.

When Rudyard Kipling wrote in *Puck of Pook's Hill*:

Of all the trees that grow so fair,
Old England to adorn,
Greater are none beneath the Sun
Than Oak and Ash and Thorn

...he had a fair point.

Sources:
Dunstall, Malcolm, 'Oak, Ash and Thorn' in *Wiþowinde* 14 (1969)
Kemble, John, *Anglo-Saxon Runes* (1991)
Pollington, Stephen, *Rudiments of Runelore* (1995)

Originally published in Lyra 17, Samhain 2014

Whispers of the Web: the Anglo-Saxon Futhorc

L AST time, I focused in detail on five Anglo-Saxon runes relating to tree lore. I'm now going to zoom out and present the Anglo-Saxon Futhorc as a whole.

The amount we know for sure about Anglo-Saxon rune magic is pretty scant. It was only a few centuries ago that anyone realised that the Anglo-Saxons had their own runes at all: runes were previously assumed to be a purely Scandinavian and German phenomenon, and a bias towards 'Norse' runes persists to this day. Surviving examples of native English rune inscriptions are comparatively few, and most that do survive are on stone monuments from the Christian era, such as the Ruthwell Cross.

Unlike some Scandinavian countries though, where runes were banished by the Church who saw them as a pagan abomination, the early English Church happily adopted and embraced them; there's even a runic inscription on the coffin of St. Cuthbert in Durham Cathedral. Most surviving examples are in stone, a long-lived medium, but it's probable that the majority of Anglo-Saxon rune carvings were done on wood. Nothing remains of these today, but we do have the runes themselves, and their basic meanings, and our ancestral connections to English myth and magic. As the runes enshrine universal principles they are as potent today as they were 1500 years ago.

If you're already familiar with the runes of the Elder Futhark, the most commonly used system today, you will recognise a lot of the Anglo-Saxon runes, though perhaps with a few changes and variations. Many are exactly the same but others have altered shapes. In most cases the shapes are designed to bring all the runes up to full stave height, with more consistent proportions. In addition, the rune which is used as a letter 'a' in the Elder Futhark becomes an 'o' in the Anglo-Saxon version, which is why it's called the Futhorc. But there are also some completely new symbols which aren't found elsewhere.

While the Elder Futhark contains 24 runes, the Anglo-Saxon Futhorc expands this basic set to 32, plus or minus one or two Northumbrian variations. Thirty-two is the most practical number from a magical point of view, because all rune alphabets are divided into *aettir*, or groups of eight (*aett* = singular, *aettir* = plural). The Elder Futhark has three *aettir* and the Anglo-Saxon Futhorc has four. This is one of the compelling reasons to use the Saxon Futhorc: the extra runes add new colours to its palette, giving it more subtlety of expression than the Elder Futhark.

As with the Tarot, it's possible to use the runes as a bog standard divination tool and simply rote-learn the "meanings", but the most powerful way to use them is to open yourself to them intuitively and learn to understand the universal principles expressed through them. And like the Tarot, the new agey fortune-tellery type stuff is a mere shadow of what the system is capable of. Each rune represents an archetypal principle, an expression of the created world or human experience. Taken together they provide a framework for making sense of the universe.

Knowing where to start is the main issue, and for that we had best look at some of the mythology of the Anglo-Saxon people. In an earlier article I briefly touched on the concept of Wyrd, a universal energy of fate or destiny which controls and connects all things and is visualised as a vast three-dimensional web. It has much in common with the concept of Awen, and also fits remarkably well with the standard model of particle physics. The recently confirmed existence of the Higgs field, an energy field occupying the entire universe which is responsible for interacting with particles and causing them to acquire mass – a fundamental process of Creation – is not that dissimilar to the concept of Wyrd, at least in general principle. But there is also a sense in which Wyrd acts like Karma, running through the affairs of mankind and bringing back to them what they deserve.

In the Saxon worldview, the gods are subject to Wyrd as much as humans are, as it represents the energetic substance underpinning the whole of Creation, including the Otherworld and the as yet unmanifest. It is considered very fluid and dynamic, so although it represents the workings of Fate, it's very much an interactive process which can be directed and manipulated. Every action is mirrored back. The force behind the Web of Wyrd is the interaction

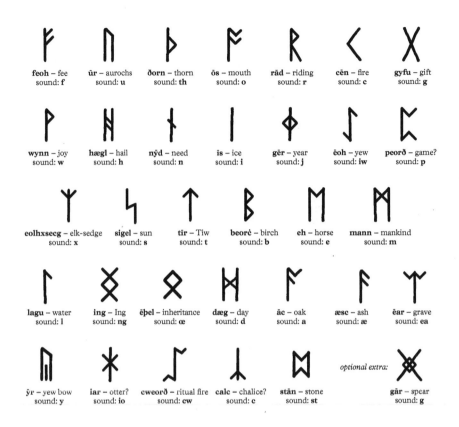

feoh – fee
sound: **f**

ûr – aurochs
sound: **u**

ðorn – thorn
sound: **th**

ôs – mouth
sound: **o**

râd – riding
sound: **r**

cên – fire
sound: **c**

gyfu – gift
sound: **g**

wynn – joy
sound: **w**

hægl – hail
sound: **h**

nŷd – need
sound: **n**

îs – ice
sound: **i**

gêr – year
sound: **j**

êoh – yew
sound: **iw**

peorð – game?
sound: **p**

eolhxsecg – elk-sedge
sound: **x**

sigel – sun
sound: **s**

tîr – Tiw
sound: **t**

beorċ – birch
sound: **b**

eh – horse
sound: **e**

mann – mankind
sound: **m**

lagu – water
sound: **l**

ing – Ing
sound: **ng**

êþel – inheritance
sound: **œ**

dæg – day
sound: **d**

âc – oak
sound: **a**

æsc – ash
sound: **æ**

êar – grave
sound: **ea**

ŷr – yew bow
sound: **y**

iar – otter?
sound: **io**

cweorð – ritual fire
sound: **cw**

calc – chalice?
sound: **c**

stân – stone
sound: **st**

optional extra:

gâr – spear
sound: **g**

of the two polarised primal energies, Fire and Ice. Fire is in a state of constant change and movement, consuming or altering everything it touches. Ice is frozen and static, preventing change or movement in whatever it touches. Fire expands, ice contracts. All creation emerges from the meeting of these two opposite principles. Once these concepts are understood, the dynamic behind the runes easily falls into place.

Also within the Anglo-Saxon cosmology is the division of existence into three levels, the Upper, Middle and Lower realms. This idea is by no means limited to the Anglo-Saxons so it's a concept we're very familiar with. In our physical lives we occupy the middle or surface world, with the spiritual world of the starry heavens above us and the underworld of inner earth below us. And of course these worlds mirror one another: as above, so below. When the permutations of mirroring are taken into account, we have three groups of three – which gives us the magical number nine. This is readily visualised in a grid of nine rods.

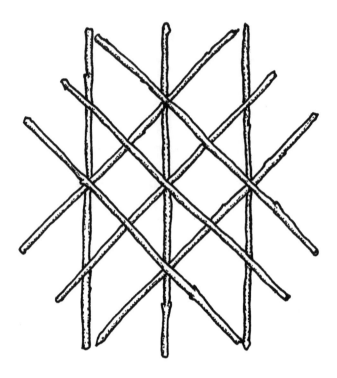

The 'Nine Glory-Twigs' of Woden form a glyph which represents both the World Tree and the Web of Wyrd. It is the key to understanding the runes, all of which are contained within it.

Nine was a very important number in Anglo-Saxon culture. It crops up over and over again in their stories, poems, charms and spells. The 10th century text known as the *Lacnunga* gives us the famous Nine Herbs Charm, ostensibly a spell for healing but which actually has meanings on many different levels. At the culmination of this, the spirit of an adder appears and the god Woden comes along and strikes it with "nine glory-twigs" or rods, causing it to fly into nine pieces.

> *A worm came crawling, it bit a person,*
> *Then Woden took up nine glory-twigs,*
> *Struck the adder then so it flew into nine parts.*

It's not defined exactly what glory-twigs are, but there are many reasons to assume they are either rune-staves or sticks for empowering runes. Woden is the god who presides over runes, having acquired them and brought them into the world through hanging on the World Tree for nine nights (and it should be pointed out that Woden's powers of healing and runelore continued to be used by the English long after England was Christianised). There is also a connection between snakes and rune magic, because many runic monuments show the runes written along the body of a snake. Sweden is full of examples of this on runestones which date

Serpent motif on a Viking runestone at Grällsta, Västmanland, Sweden.

Swedish National Heritage Board

from this period. It's as if the snake is the medium on which the runes are laid out, and the striking with nine rods empowers them by releasing their powers into their nine component parts.

Which brings us back to the grid of nine glory-twigs. This glyph is quite fundamental and will bring many insights to the study of runes. We see three groups of three sticks arranged in symmetry. Three stand upright in the centre, three are placed diagonally from left to right, and three diagonally from right to left. The central group of three represents our earthly plane of existence, what the Saxons called the Middle Enclosure. The other two represent the sky realm and the underworld realm, although which way round they are depends on which way you're looking at them. All three groups reach through all three realms, because everything is reflected in an 'as above, so below' relationship.

If this doesn't seem obvious at first glance, it soon pops into perspective in a meditative setting. There is a visible line of symmetry down the vertical rod in the centre, and an invisible line of symmetry going horizontally through the middle, at right angles to the vertical rod. The relationship between these visible and invisible symmetries, and the central point at which they intersect, is also fruitful for meditation. Taken as a whole, this glyph can be used in a similar way to the Qabalistic Tree of Life, and used as a kind of map of the universe. Although it has a different layout and structure from the Tree of Life and should not be regarded as directly equivalent, its patterns of interconnecting paths serve a very similar purpose.

As a 'Tree of Life' it becomes a way of making sense of another Anglo-Saxon mythological concept, the World Tree. The best known form of this myth is the Norse version, the Yggdrasil, the cosmic ash tree which interconnects the 'nine worlds'. The Anglo-Saxon version is slightly different (not least because the Saxon cosmology involves seven planes rather than nine) and is known as the Irminsul. This vast pillar or tree is seen as the central beam or pivot at the centre of Creation. Its top reaches through the starry heavens to the primordial Ice. Its roots reach through the deep earth to the primordial Fire.

Unlike the Yggdrasil, the English version is a yew. It was on this great, powerful, cosmic yew tree, whose roots and branches stretch beyond human imagining, that the god Woden underwent an initiation process, wounded with a spear and hanging for nine nights, before finding and snatching the runes and bringing their knowledge through to the human world. The long-lived, evergreen yew tree with its connections to the Otherworld and its tradition of transformative shamanic experience is the obvious candidate for the Irminsul.

Our grid of nine glory-twigs, being a representation of the World Tree, contains the lore and power of all of the runes. I say this because of the remarkable fact that the shapes of all the runes can be found within it. Yes, all of them. Try it!

This is how Woden's ninefold experience yields the rune wisdom in its entirety; the runes all exist within this ninefold grid simultaneously, and can be drawn out by shifting your consciousness from one to another. It's also the reason the Anglo-Saxon people were able to expand the range of runes beyond the common 24 symbols of the Futhark – they found new symbols within the same grid pattern, symbols which have as much validity as the earlier runes because they came from the same source. This also of course raises the possibility that there are more runes there to be discovered, and that you can find them yourself, simply by picking them out of the grid.

It follows that the shapes of the runes are significant, though perhaps not in the way the modern mind wants to assume. They are all angular in form and contain no curves; they also contain no *horizontal* lines, only verticals and diagonals. The usual explanation for this is that it makes them easier to carve, and is particularly well suited to carving on wood. This makes perfect practical sense, but it's no coincidence that the grid pattern from which the runes are derived is similarly angular with no horizontals.

There have been many attempts to interpret primitive pictograms from the shapes of the runes to explain their symbolism, such as equating the two upward prongs of the first rune, **feoh** ᚠ, with the horns of a cow, since 'cattle' is one of its possible meanings. But this doesn't hold up, because it works for some runes more than others, and some make no pictorial sense no matter how contrived and convoluted the efforts. This is too modern a way of looking at it. Again, our grid of nine glory-twigs provides us with an alternative answer, one which is more subtle and more profound.

The fact that the runes are made up from two (and only two) types of line is highly significant. It takes us back to our two primordial forces, Fire and Ice. The runes themselves tell us which is which. There is a rune whose name is **īs** (pronounced ice), and whose meaning is exactly that. This rune consists of a single, vertical line. Everything about it suggests stasis and rigidity. There is also a rune for fire, named **cēn**. This rune comprises two diagonal lines and no verticals, and its appearance is altogether more dynamic. Most of the other runes are made from a combination of vertical and diagonal lines, and this is where their shapes take on significance and meaning, as they represent the interactions of the forces of Fire and Ice. This simple formula enables us to reach the fundamental meaning of each rune, through its relationship to the primal polarity of Creation.

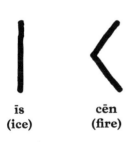

īs
(ice)

cēn
(fire)

When you look at each rune, notice how it's proportioned: whether it's top heavy, bottom heavy, balanced towards one side or the other, whether it has one or more lines of symmetry. And take note of its proportions of vertical lines (Ice) and diagonal lines (Fire).

For example, the rune **tīr** ↑ has a solid vertical line through the centre representing stability, with two diagonal lines angled together at the top, drawing dynamic forces upwards to the arrow point. This nicely sums up the spirit of this rune, whose meanings encompass a warrior's sword or spear and a celestial pointer (the Pole Star) showing the way.

The symbol **þorn** þ, on the other hand, has its dynamic diagonal lines coming out from and then going back into the vertical line, forming both a spike and an enclosed area. This fits well with the rune's variant meanings of sharp and unpleasant experiences and of protection. The rune **gyfu** X, with its long, strong diagonals, no verticals, and two axes of symmetry, is a beautifully balanced and egalitarian rune which adequately portrays the idea of a gift or exchange. Using these keys, you can reach a deep understanding of the Futhorc without any need for rote-learning, although a guide is provided at the end of this article to get you started.

How to make a set of rune staves

Making your own set of runes is one of the best ways to get to know the Futhorc properly, and mercifully it doesn't require anything much in the way of artistic or woodworking skills. You can, if you wish, make an artistic and beautiful set, but there's probably more to be said for the rough ones made from simple sticks – they feel more authentic somehow. Not just because they're more likely to be similar to what our ancestors made, but because the most important factor is working *with* the wood and allowing the character of the stick to express itself. It's a form of tree magic and the spirit of the wood is more important than the uniformity of the finished result. There's no right or wrong way to make them, and no standard size or style, but the following is a guide to how I made mine.

The first thing to decide is what kind of wood to make them from. There's nothing to stop you just picking up any unidentified stick you find, but given the magical properties of different trees, it's nice to make them from something appropriate. Yew is a good choice: it's the sacred tree of the Irminsul and thus the mythological source

of the Saxon runes, and its lovely dense creamy wood carves well –
although it is very hard and waxy, so you need a sharp knife and a
bit more patience with the pyrography iron. Apple wood has a nice
Avalonian connection, while hazel is a tree traditionally associated
with divination and wisdom. You don't have to make them all
from the same wood though; you can use a mixture, random or
otherwise. One option is to use the five trees which appear in the
Futhorc itself: yew, birch, oak, ash, thorn. Or a pairing of holly and
oak. Or go for nine sacred trees for the full 'glory-twigs' experience.

For my set, I decided to use four types of wood, one for each
aett, collected from the grounds of Hawkwood where the Gareth
Knight Group was founded – including some from a magnificent
ancient sycamore which grows over a spring. The others I selected
were ash, yew and elm, though this choice was dictated by what
was available as much as magical symbolism. I then found myself
forced into a rethink when the elm I'd collected turned out not to
be enough to make a complete *aett*, so I supplemented it with some
thorn wood collected from a powerful faery hawthorn on one of my
favourite local hills. This makes a right old hotchpotch of different

woods, some with bark on and some without, but it really doesn't seem to matter.

1. Collect your pieces of wood. They don't have to be perfect, but try to select sticks which are of a uniform size and diameter, reasonably straight, without too many knots. Mine are about half an inch in diameter. I prefer to pick up seasoned sticks which have fallen naturally rather than cutting them direct from the tree, but you can do either. Old sticks will dry out quicker, though you have to watch that they aren't rotten. You can however use sticks which are spalted (shot through with tiny black lines of fungus), which

look very decorative. Leave them to dry for two weeks or so.

2. After cleaning off any dirt or loose bark, saw your sticks into 32 pieces, keeping them all roughly the same length. A mitre box is very handy for getting the ends straight. They can be any length you want: mine are just over two inches, but you could make one-inch ones if you want them very compact for divination use, or four inches if you want proper staves large enough to hold in your hand.

3. Using a sharp wood-carving knife, slice a flat surface in the side of the stick. I just did a simple oval window in the middle, but you can cut a

slice near the end of the stave if you want to have the rune at the top, or even slice the entire side flat. If necessary, you can chamfer the top and bottom of the stave, though I didn't bother to. Whether you leave the bark on or strip it off is a matter of preference. If it's loose and flaky then it's best removed, but if it's firmly attached then it looks very nice left on.

4. The runes can be burned onto the surface of the stick using a pyrography iron. If you don't have a purpose-made one, a soldering iron should do the job. You could paint the symbols on as an alternative, but this might be less durable if the sticks are to have a lot of handling. The finished staves can be left as they are without any sealant, but if you want them to last longer you can use an oil to seal them. Beware of smelly commercial timber preservatives which will make them unpleasant to handle. The simplest option is to use ordinary culinary walnut oil (not toasted!) to flood the surface, then wipe off the excess and leave them to dry for a few days. The wood should absorb all the oil. You can leave it at that, or finish off with a beeswax polish. Another option is just to use polyurethane varnish, which gives good protection, but it looks a bit synthetic.

Once finished, you can make or buy a suitable bag to keep them in. Simple, undyed linen or hemp drawstring bags seem to go well with them, or if you're feeling adventurous you can boil up some woad and dye it yourself!

Sources:
Most of the information on Anglo-Saxon cosmology in this article comes from
 Linsell, Tony, *Anglo-Saxon Runes*, Anglo-Saxon Books, 1992.
Translation based on Pollington, Stephen, *Leechcraft: Early English Charms, Plantlore and Healing*, Anglo-Saxon Books, 2000.
For more explanation of this formula, see Lilly, Simon H., *Rune Equations*, Tree
 Seer Books, 2014.

Originally published in Lyra 18, Imbolc 2015

ᚠ	*Fee. Goods, moveable wealth, cattle. Status and wealth maintained through sharing it around.*
ᚢ	*Aurochs (ox). Strength and vitality. Practical strength. Courage and capability.*
ᚦ	*Thorn. Discomfort and danger, caution, sharpness. Protection, defence. A warning not to linger.*
ᚩ	*Mouth. Communication, speech, language, news, gossip, learning. Getting the message across.*
ᚱ	*Riding. The act of planning a journey and carrying it out. Proceeding on an anticipated course.*
ᚲ	*Torch, fire. Illumination, light, knowledge. 'Seeing the light'. Comforting, homely hearthfire.*
ᚷ	*Gift. Exchange. Love. Relationship and partnership. Reciprocation. Generosity.*
ᚹ	*Joy. Enthusiasm and pleasure. Positive change. Encouragement. Harmony with the world.*
ᚻ	*Hail. Unexpected challenges. Forces of nature. Temporary disruption. Sudden change.*
ᚾ	*Need. Corrective action. Necessity. The unavoidable. Rescue. Caution and a wait-and-see approach.*
ᛁ	*Ice. Freezing and inertia. Lack of movement. Stasis, contraction, focus. Do not proceed.*
ᛄ	*Year of seasons. Harvest. Cycles and tides. Things happening in their proper time and place.*
ᛇ	*Yew. Protection, longevity, survival. Hope. Slow change. Guardianship. Re-awakening.*
ᛈ	*Game piece [?] Secrets and mysteries. Hidden knowledge. Revelation.*
ᛉ	*Elk-sedge. Success through skill and danger through ignorance.*
ᛋ	*Sun. Brightness and positivity. Warmth, energy, success. Good luck. Adventure.*
ᛏ	*Tiw (the sky god). Guidance, motivation, power, justice. Navigation by the Pole Star. Victory.*
ᛒ	*Birch. Beauty, lightness, airy movement, freshness, vitality. Growth. Creativity. New beginnings.*

ᛗ	*Horse. Movement. Transition from one state or place to another. Change. Journey. Cooperation.*
ᛘ	*Mankind. Humanity. Companionship. Mortality and life cycles. Community and contacts.*
ᛚ	*Water, lake. Intuition. Things unconscious or below the surface. Cleansing. Fluidity. Feelings.*
ᛝ	*Ing (an ancestral god). Potential. Achievement. Fruition. Expansion and completion. A sign or beacon.*
ᛞ	*Day. Dawn, brightness. Cycle of life. Optimism and positive transformation. Increase.*
ᛟ	*Inherited wealth. Heirloom. Ancestral home or lands. Static, immovable possessions. Identity, belonging.*
ᚪ	*Oak. Masculine energy and strength. Royalty and authority. Reliability and patience. Endurance.*
ᚫ	*Ash. Flexible and adaptable. Inspiration and receipt of higher knowledge. Swift energy, sure of purpose.*
ᚣ	*Dust, grave. Ending. Mortality. Closure. Dissolution. Reform. Eternity.*
ᛁ	*Yew-bow. Useful artefact made with skill. Focus and control. Concentration. Application of will.*
ᛇ	*Otter, beaver, water beast. Happy-go-lucky lack of worry. Lack of attachment. Acceptance. Equanimity.*
ᛂ	*Ritual fire. Sacred flame. Letting go. Unblocking of energy. Transformation and purification.*
ᛣ	*Chalice/chalk. Remembrance. Ancestral connection. [The original meaning of this rune is uncertain.]*
ᛥ	*Stone. Stability and solidity. Crystallisation into matter and form. A state of being earthed and rooted.*
ᚸ	*Spear [?] The symbol of Woden on the World Tree.*

Joseph of Arimathea, Fisher King

A magical interlude in the
13th century poem *Sone de Nansay*

with translations by Gareth Knight

ONE of the intriguing things sometimes found in early literature is the appearance of an unexplained magical interlude which seems to spring out of nowhere, as if aimed at a different audience; a bit like the Groundlings scenes in Shakespeare's plays, only with esoteric rather than comedy value. Within certain medieval stories can be found spine-tinglingly magical episodes which almost seem to have been chucked randomly into otherwise mundane and straightforward texts.

Such detours often take the form of a sea journey, in which the characters visit a mysterious island which is clearly otherworldly in nature.

One good example of this is the 14th century French text *Le Bâtard de Bouillon (The Bastard of Bouillon)* which chunters on for some while about the Crusades before being interrupted by a strange interlude where the protagonists land on a magical island full of apple trees and surrounded by clouds, where they meet King Artus and his sister Morgue. In this vivid portrayal of the otherworldly Isle of Avalon, the characters have to discover the true flower of Christian knighthood by plucking a rose which is under guard by two armed automatons in Artus's magical garden. A further test involves a horn of ivory and they are finally presented with a white horse – both obvious faery symbols – before the narrative goes back to business as usual, i.e. some light fratricide and bashing somebody's head in with a chessboard. So why does the narrative suddenly nip into the realm of Faery and out again? It's never explained.

A similarly incongruous magical interlude can be found in an obscure 13th century epic poem called *Sone de Nansay*, a hefty text which mostly comprises the military and romantic exploits of the crusading hero Sone (a possible historical character) and his descendants, but also contains a curious detour into pure Grail territory via a sea journey. In preparation for a military adventure with the King of Norway, Sone is taken to a curious island inhabited by twelve monks in a castle. The community was founded by Joseph of Arimathea, who built the castle to house the Grail Hallows. There follows a remarkable description of this Grail Castle and the role of Joseph as the king, after which Sone is shown the Grail before sailing onward to a life of macho exploits.

I first came across *Sone de Nansay* as part of my study of another early Grail text, *Perlesvaus*, because it has been suggested (by R.S. Loomis)[1] that these two works, along with the Welsh *mabinogi* of *Branwen*, are all similar enough that they must be derived from a common source, presumed to be a (now lost) earlier text. Personally I'm not wholly convinced that they are based on another text; it seems more likely to me that their authors were independently writing down their take on the Grail lore that was common currency at the time. With great respect for Grail scholarship, I think the academic focus on fitting every text into a hierarchy of other works (relying almost solely on a chronology of known, surviving texts) can be incredibly limiting. We will never definitively know the origins of these tales, and you really have to be prepared to trust your intuition with mythological material, otherwise the crock of gold soon turns into a bag of dead leaves.

The Grail material in *Sone de Nansay* is brief and undoubtedly off-message as far as the usual Grail narrative is concerned. It has no Arthurian content, and no quests or Grail winners. There's nothing to say that it's anything more than an aberration amid the bulk of Grail literature. But that's exactly why it interests me, because I've noticed that any text which doesn't conform to the common consensus on the Arthurian/Grail story tends to get marginalised, discredited and forgotten. Which is a shame, because sometimes it's the obscure, ignored and 'heretical' Grail texts which have the most enlightening nuggets of deep magic within them.

So having read about the *Sone* poem in Loomis's book I was naturally keen to have a closer look at it, but I immediately ran into a problem. The text is so little known and little read, it's never been translated into English. The only edition I could find was a translation into modern French,[2] printed alongside the original medieval text. My French isn't that good so I had to turn to my friendly neighbourhood medieval French scholar (i.e. Gareth Knight), who kindly translated the relevant section for me. The Grail interlude is only a short section, and begins around verse 4300 of the text, at a point in the story where the young Sone de Nansay is embarking on a dangerous military quest with King Alain of Norway.

Given the dangers they will face, King Alain decides to take Sone first to a place where he can make confession and hear the word of God. They set off with around twenty companions and travel for two days through strange mountainous lands. On the third day they set off at midnight (the liminal time) and arrive at their destination on the sea shore at midday (ditto), in a bay between two great rocks. This is supposedly the site of a great causeway leading across the sea, but we are told that "it was difficult to find and many valiant knights had come to grief without ever discovering the place" – giving us a hint of the Otherworld. However, on this occasion the causeway is impassable, because the sea is covering its rocky path.

King Alain sounds his horn at the waterside, and very quickly a boat appears, rowed by two monks. Sone and Alain are invited into the boat and the monks row them across the sea until they come to a castle:

> ... it was situated in the open sea in such a way that no catapult could launch projectiles on it and no war machine could be constructed that could do anything to damage it, for it was built on a natural rock surrounded by sea, its crenellated walls rising up from the rock. On the exterior wall were four towers, which were, in my view, the best in the world. In the middle of the four towers was a great one that surpassed the others. This tower constituted the palace; there had never been built anything more sumptuous. It was 100 feet wide in every direction, for it was perfectly circular. Exactly in the middle was a chimney founded on four gilded pillars that supported a great pure copper pipe crossing the reception hall at four feet in height; this pipe was decorated on the outside with gold coloured mosaics. Such was the interior of the palace, never had any more sumptuous been constructed. [4398]

This scene has a resonance with Grail Castles in other texts. It bears a particular resemblance to a scene near the end of *Perlesvaus*, where the hero is carried away by a ship and arrives at a four-towered castle in the sea.

Here in this tale, Sone de Nansay and King Alain disembark at the castle and are greeted by a community of twelve monks, plus an abbot, who represent the direct spiritual lineage of Joseph of Arimathea. As it is lunchtime, Sone and the king are invited to join the monks for an *al fresco* meal, where they are able to admire both the local wildlife and the curious spectacle of mechanical 'wind-chime' leopards mounted on the perimeter wall:

They put the table in a covered courtyard, the finest they had ever seen. It overhung the walls and gave onto the sea, but was surrounded by a pretty low wall of white marble; there was not a bird, animal or fish that was not represented there. It was very pleasant to see; and on the walls were ten leopards, each with its mouth gaping; an ingenious system made them turn so that their mouths were always facing the wind. When the wind blew, each one made a harmonious and different sound, so agreeable to hear that no one could tire of it. It would never be tiresome to anyone in good health. And whoever looked out over the sea from there could never find a scene more beautiful. [4466]

From the other side one could see the forest full of laburnum and cypress, sycamore and alisier, almond and olives and other beautiful trees were found in this forest near the sea. There one could see stags at play and the fallow deer come and go, with swans, peacocks, falcons, great diving birds that had wings but could not fly well and had to have both fresh and salt water. I will tell you what they looked like, for no one has ever seen one. According to my judgment they are as big as a badger, and I am sure not any smaller. They are similar to bats, for their wings have a veritable fur. They possess much hair and a pointed muzzle and ceaselessly make such a racket that the whole forest rings with it. [4488]

At the castle three streams of water meet which well up from the rock and fall into the sea, the fresh water mixing with the salt sea. There were so many fish gathered there that they could never be destroyed simply by fishing. One could explore the whole world without ever finding so strong a castle or one provided with such riches. [4500]

The following day, Sone and Alain attend mass at the monks' church where they see the coffin which contains the body of Joseph of Arimathea. The abbot then relates the story of how Joseph of Arimathea came to establish the castle. At first this follows the familiar story given to us in other sources such as the Vulgate Cycle. It tells how Joseph was imprisoned and left for dead, but was visited by Christ who gave him the Grail, and how the Grail nourished him so that after 40 years he was found alive and well in a cavern filled with light. So far, so familiar. It's after the release of Joseph from this imprisonment that the story takes a very different turn.

In the *Sone de Nansay* version, Joseph retrieves with his own hands the other half of the Grail Hallows, the spear of Longinus, which has been buried within a wall. Taking his two precious magical objects with him, he is carried off to sea on a ship "moving without mast or sail" until he lands at the shore of an island. A horse and knight's armour are ready waiting for him, and he assumes the life of a warrior, where he gets up to all kinds of derring-do including driving all the Saracens out of Norway (!) and killing its pagan king. The king has a very beautiful young daughter who Joseph falls in love with and wants to take in marriage, very much against her will, as she naturally isn't very keen on a man who has just slaughtered all her family and friends. The one obstacle to their marriage is that she is an unrepentant pagan who refuses to accept Christianity, but Joseph has her forcibly baptised, and duly marries her.

Meanwhile, God is a bit put out by all this and decides that Joseph needs to be punished. And so God wounds him "in the small of the back and below", leaving him physically incapacitated and in such pain that he can do nothing but lie down, unable even to use his limbs. And thus he remains for the rest of his life. We are told that he lived a very long and holy life in devoted service to Christ, and that he and his bride were crowned king and queen, and that Joseph loved his wife very deeply and suffered the constant pain of his wounds for her sake.

It should be noted that the reason God is so cheesed off is not because Joseph has forced the girl into marriage after murdering her father, but because the marriage is tainted by sin – since she is still at heart a pagan and a non-believer despite the outward appearance of baptism. Such a view is par for the course in the 13th century!

It's shortly after becoming king that Joseph builds the castle on top of the rock in the sea. Its location is special not just because it's naturally fortified by the sea, but because of the pure freshwater streams which tumble down around its walls, "so that there was a profusion of fish of all kinds":

> *The good king had a boat, and after he had attended mass he could board it and go fishing. With him was a sailor who always took the boat to places he wanted to go. Thus fishing, and company of the sailors, pleased him; here he forgot his terrible suffering, for he endured such pain as would have killed many men. And because he fished like that, his nickname spread everywhere: he was called the 'fisher king' and his name is still famous. He lived this life for many days until a knight should come to cure him.* [4832]

Now things are getting very interesting. It couldn't really be more clear that in this text, even if not in any other Grail story, Joseph of Arimathea is the Fisher King. He is wounded in the nether regions and can only be healed by the arrival of a particular knight. Also included is the usual Grail motif of the Wasteland, where the king's incapacity also afflicts the land and its people. The text goes on:

> *His country is called Logres today, and that is established truth. Logres is a name of suffering, known for tears and weeping. It is known for suffering because they sowed neither peas nor wheat, no child was born there, no young girl married, no tree grew leaves, no field became green, no bird had fledglings, no beasts had young, and the king was mutilated until he had expiated his sins, for Jesus Christ was greatly angered by the commerce of Joseph with the miscreant.* [4860]

Having related the story of how Joseph of Arimathea founded the castle and its community of monks, the abbot blesses Sone and tells him he will show him the Grail, which is still kept at the castle.

> *The abbot gave his blessing and accorded them his plenary indulgence. He then opened an ivory reliquary ornamented with many sculpted scenes, and took from it the holy Graal. The whole place was illuminated. At that moment you could have seen the*

monks weep and in tears loudly sing the Te Deum Laudamus. There do not exist more such receptacles. On the altar, near the cross, the Graal was placed by the holy man and friend of God. He then brought the holy lance of which you have heard me speak. The abbot and his monks wept so much that one would have thought they were made of tears. The iron of the lance was magnificent and shining. At its point, before them, a drop of red blood formed, at which many marvelled. The abbot showed them two reliquaries, in one reposed the body of Joseph and in the other his son Adam. Joseph only had two sons. The older was named Josephé and was the first consecrated bishop. Protected by these relics, the abbot honoured God first and the relics afterwards. The monks and he served with zeal. When the abbot had shown all, he removed the robes with which he had sung the mass, took the young man by the hand and said: "Come now, my friend, you have fasted long enough. It is now midday. Go and restore yourself, for you will have much need of it." [4938]

And so the Grail episode draws to a close, as Sone and King Alain take a final hearty meal with the monks before sailing back the way they came. Their adventure then sees them heading to the port of Saint-Joseph in Norway – supposedly the place where Joseph of Arimathea had entered Norway many centuries before. In case you're wondering, no, I'm not aware of any other legend which claims that Joseph of Arimathea visited Norway! But then, it all depends what you mean by Norway.

The central thrust of R.S. Loomis's argument is that *Sone de Nansay* preserves the ancient Welsh legend of Brân in one of its purest and most primitive forms. His explanation is worth reading in full but for our immediate purposes, let's just say that there appears to be Welsh-Celtic material underlying this French poem, as is the case with many other medieval Grail texts. Somewhere along the line the story has been derived from Welsh sources. Loomis notes that the Welsh name for Norway is *Llychlyn*, and then cites Sir John Rhys's claim that the original meaning of Llychlyn was "the fabulous land beneath the lakes or waves of the sea".[3] If this is true, then the references to Norway in *Sone de Nansay* may not have anything to do with the outer plane nation of Norway but rather it may be a reference to the well-established Celtic Otherworld of *Tír fo Thuinn*, the Land under Wave. Obviously this casts this whole episode of our story in a completely different light! King Alain of Norway suddenly becomes a potential Faery King.

If there has been a confusion between Llychlyn–Scandinavia and Llychlyn–Otherworld, it presumably happened quite a long time ago, as there are other medieval authors who make similar head-scratching references to Norway, including Geoffrey of Monmouth, who refers to Brennius marrying the King of Norway's daughter[4] (which closely parallels the marriage of Joseph of Arimathea to the King of Norway's daughter in *Sone de Nansay*). The mention of a Norwegian port called Saint-Joseph doesn't seem to have any basis in the real world, as far as I can tell, but if we accept the interpretation of 'Norway' as a non-physical realm then it becomes a reference to Joseph of Arimathea entering the Otherworld; again, not part of the conventional narrative but it's not a million miles away from his legendary association with the inner/outer realms of Avalon.

We're told that Joseph of Arimathea settled in the land of Logres, which is clearly a reference to England. This certainly ties in nicely with the established medieval legend that Joseph brought the Grail hallows to England. Later in the poem we are given a name for the island on which the Grail Castle stands: *Galoche* (Wales). Clearly the island isn't large enough to be England or Wales in any real sense; it's basically only big enough to host the great castle and an area of forest. The forest includes almond and olive trees, neither of which is native to Great Britain. We're also given a description of the wildlife, which has been identified as deer, swans, peacocks and diver-ducks;[5] again, not quite the English pastoral scene. Could the author of the poem have been ignorant of England's geography and wildlife? Perhaps, but in the poem as a whole he shows a pretty good grasp of realistic detail. So again we're looking at the innerworld manifestation of Logres rather than the physical land of England.

There are other details to back this up, not least the description of the causeway under the sea which provides the sole route to the island, accessible only to a few. This is a motif which crops up a lot in Grail legends as a 'crossing-over' point to convey the questor into the realm of Faery, often available only under certain conditions. It makes sense in this context that the journey undertaken by Sone and King Alain is a journey into the Otherworld, or rather a deeper level of the Otherworld if we're assuming that 'Norway' is not physical either. All the activity takes place at the two 'crossing-over' times, noon or midnight. However, while the sea is covering the causeway, as it is here, then it's not possible for the questor to make their own journey: the call has to be sounded and a response awaited. In this case, King Alain uses the time-honoured method of blowing a horn – that perennial tool for summoning the denizens of Faery – and the ferrymen duly come out across the sea to fetch him.

And the scene at the castle resonates strongly with the other 'heretical' Grail text *Perlesvaus*, where the Grail Castle is staffed by a community of twelve ageless knights (rather than monks), and the body of Joseph of Arimathea is likewise preserved in a special tomb. The main difference is that in *Perlesvaus*, the tomb of Joseph of Arimathea (whose identity is not revealed until near the end) is not in the Grail Castle itself but keeps popping up in various locations associated with the Grail, guarded by disembodied voices which warn any casual prodder that the tomb must not be touched by anyone except the "good knight" (i.e. the destined Grail winner). When this ordained time comes, the tomb will open to reveal the identity of its occupant. Thus, the tomb of Joseph of Arimathea is central to the Grail mystery in both texts, differing only in context details.

That there is something significant in the company of twelve who guard the Grail, there can be little doubt. It's a theme which can also be found in the *Queste del Saint Graal*, which features twelve knights who are served by the Grail in the castle of the Maimed King. The question "Whom does it serve?" is very pertinent here: who are the twelve companions?

In *Sone de Nansay* we are told that there are twelve monks in the castle because that was the number of Christ's disciples, but that's all it says about them. In *Perlesvaus* we're also given no information about the identity of the twelve knights in the Grail Castle, but their role is very much connected to the testing of the potential Grail winner. When Sir Gawain arrives at the Grail Castle they host a feast for him during which the Grail is paraded in and out three times; they try hard to prompt him to respond but he neglects to ask the crucial question, after which they pack up the feast and leave him to his fate. The big difference in *Sone de Nansay* is that it omits the questing and testing. The twelve companions and the feast are there, but there are no Knights of the Round Table in this poem and no Faery damsels laying down challenges. Instead the abbot is happy to wheel out the Grail and the Spear for Sone to marvel at, without putting him through any spiritual test. Perhaps this is the post-Perceval condition at the Grail Castle, and we're to assume it's no longer necessary for such tests to be applied once the true Grail winner has blazed the trail.

Let us return to *Perlesvaus* for a moment and see how it sets out its version of the legend. We are told right at the start of the text[6] that Perlesvaus (Perceval) himself is descended from Joseph of Arimathea, who is his mother's uncle. This makes no sense from a historical point of view, as it's hardly possible for a woman living in King Arthur's time to be Joseph of Arimathea's niece, but we're not dealing with a normal physical lineage here. Perlesvaus's mother has three brothers, so of course Joseph of Arimathea is uncle to them too. They are all Faery kings of one kind or another, the principle among them being the Fisher King. So the destined Grail winner Perlesvaus is the nephew of the Fisher King, and the Fisher King is the nephew of Joseph of Arimathea!

We are also told Perlesvaus's lineage on his father's side. His father is a knight named Alain le Gros, who is the eldest of twelve brothers. All of the brothers are knights, and all of them serve for a period of twelve years before dying in battle. They have curious faery-like names: Galerian of the White Tower, Fortimes of the Crimson Heath, Meralis of the Field of Silks.

Although the details are different between *Perlesvaus* and *Sone de Nansay*, there is clearly something going on with the number twelve! The fact that Perlesvaus's (faery?) father is called Alain, the name of the king in *Sone de Nansay*, can be seen as coincidental until you consider that there is also a character called Alain in the *Estoire del Saint Graal* who becomes the Grail guardian. I'm not necessarily suggesting that they're all the same person, but it's an intriguing example of how the Grail myth derives from the same ball of jumbled strands extruded in different directions.

While *Perlesvaus* has Joseph of Arimathea as the Fisher King's uncle, *Sone de Nansay* has Joseph as the Fisher King himself. This, as we have discussed, is probably unique. In every other sense the role of the Fisher King in *Sone de Nansay* broadly matches the other Grail legends.

It could be said that the confusion over the identities of archetypal figures is inherent in the Grail mythos: the Fisher King and the Maimed King are sometimes the same person or sometimes brothers, and any attempt to explain him/them in definitive terms is doomed to be swaddled in the faery mists. These are, after all, legends which are supposed to speak to us on a deep imaginative level rather than to make sense in purely rational terms. But there is one crucial advantage in *Sone de Nansay*'s identification of Joseph of Arimathea as the Fisher King and Grail guardian, and that is that *it forges a direct lineage between Christ and the heart of the Grail mystery.*

To some extent *Perlesvaus* does the same thing, one step removed, by establishing Joseph of Arimathea as the uncle of the Grail guardian, who is in turn the uncle of the destined Grail winner. The link between the Grail mystery and the Christian mystery is implied in other texts, but is not made so explicit; it tends to leave unanswered questions about why and how the Grail Hallows ended up in Britain (or its Faery counterpart). By connecting the legend of Joseph of Arimathea's journey to Logres with the enigmatic figure of the Fisher King, whose kingship is so deeply rooted in the land that the land suffers the same loss of fertility from his unhealed wound, a powerful and fruitful coherence emerges from the unfathomable mystery. A connection is also made between Joseph of Arimathea as a historical person and his special status as the enduring otherworldly guardian, along with the twelve Faery companions, who remains for all time at the very centre of the Grail mystery.

1   Loomis, Roger Sherman *The Grail, from Celtic Myth to Christian Symbol,* chapter 10 (Constable, 1992).
2   Lachet, Claude (trans.) *Sone de Nansay* (Honoré Champion, 2012).
3   Loomis, Roger Sherman *The Grail, from Celtic Myth to Christian Symbol,* p.144
4   Geoffrey of Monmouth *The History of the Kings of Britain* (Boydell Press, 2007).
5   Loomis, Roger Sherman *The Grail, from Celtic Myth to Christian Symbol,* p.137
6   Bryant, Nigel (trans.) *The High Book of the Grail,* p.1 (D.S.Brewer, 1978).

Originally published in Lyra 19, Beltane 2015

Brìghd in Avalon
A spark of ancestral fire in Glastonbury and beyond

L ET'S begin with an invocation. It's one I use a lot in ritual openings, and which I personally prefer to the traditional Hermetic openings. Why? Because it goes straight for the heart centre and brings in a real emotional punch which, when you get it right, is profoundly powerful and humbling, and quite unlike any other invocation I've tried. It was used a lot in the old days of the Gareth Knight Group, but it was originally channelled by R.J. Stewart.

> In the name of the Son of Light
> The Son of Maria
> Foster-son of Brìghd in Avalon
> Keystone of the Arch of Heaven
> Who joins as One the forks upholding of the sky

It's well worth reading R.J. Stewart's fantastic little book *The Arch of Heaven* which is dedicated to these verses (the above quote is just the first verse). In it, he describes how the words originally came through to him in a spirit of compassion as he sought to help somebody trapped in an after-death condition, and he gives a detailed explanation of its many levels of meaning as well as the many ways it can be used for attunement, dedication and clearing. For the purposes of this article however, I'm interested in what he has to say about just one half-line: Brìghd in Avalon.

Brìghd is one of the most complex and nuanced figures in the British Mystery Tradition (and that's saying something). Is she a saint? Is she a goddess? She is both, and at the same time she's neither, because she transcends narrow definitions. She is universal, and yet she is inherently British/Celtic. She straddles pagan and Christian traditions comfortably and rises above such artificial divisions. She has a variety of names: Bridget and Bride in England, Fraid in Wales, Brigit, Brigid, Brighid or Bríd in

Ireland and Brìghd in Scotland. The Scottish and Irish variants are a product of the different Gaelic languages and although they're spelled differently they're both pronounced 'Breed'. R.J. Stewart uses the form 'Brìghd'. I use it too, because I'm familiar with it from the invocation. None is more right or wrong than another, but I like the form Brìghd because it's most similar to the modern English *bright*. Brìghd's name encapsulates her fiery spark and is rooted in the Anglo-Saxon *bryht* (bright, shining) as well as the Gaelic forms.

In her guise as saint she is an Irish nun whose feast is the eve of Candlemas (February 1st) and who is sometimes depicted milking a cow. Her foundation at Kildare is famous for its perpetual flame, tended solely by women, which is said to have been kept alight for many centuries. She has her own style of cross, an equal-armed interwoven cross traditionally made from rushes. She got about a bit: she sailed over the sea to Wales on a clod of earth which turned into a sacred mound, and she also made it to England where she founded a cell in Glastonbury (also on a mound). Even more miraculously, she turned up in the Holy Land to serve as midwife to the Virgin Mary and foster-mother to Christ, which was quite an achievement considering she wasn't born herself until the 5th century AD.

In her pagan guise she is the goddess of Spring (and indeed of springs), whose feast is celebrated at Imbolc (February 1st again) and symbolised by all things white: snowdrops, swans, milk. She presides over creative and purifying fires of all kinds and is patron of healing, smithcraft and poetry. She is a goddess of both Sun and Moon, and as well as her Celtic credentials she encapsulates the Saxon magical principles of Fire and Ice. Her transformative powers include an ability to turn water into ale, and there is a Scottish Gaelic saying "Chuir Brìghd 'a làmh 'sa bhóla" (Brìghd put her hand into the bowl) which is thought to be a reference to this. Another important symbol of hers is the fiery arrow.

Far be it from me to disentangle these threads which have been scrambled together since ancient times; I wouldn't know where to start. I prefer to take the magician's approach and accept Brìghd (or whatever name variant you prefer) at face value, and work with what we've got, and see where it leads.

In the Gareth Knight Group we've sometimes worked with Brìghd as a representative of the Planetary Being with a special relevance to the British Isles (and Ireland). In other words, she's our native version of Gaia. That's an approach which has worked well in practical magic. She is also, because of her very particular association with these islands, one of our principal ancestral goddesses with the capacity to root us very deeply into our national lineage.

In the context of R. J. Stewart's invocation, Brìghd is an intermediary between humanity and divinity, which is where the symbolism of the midwife and foster-mother comes in. Her guiding influence helps to bring through and "humanise" the contact with the Child of Light, who is a stepped-down aspect of divinity Itself. Although the invocation draws on the folklore legend that Brìghd nurtured the infant Jesus, R.J. is careful to point out that it goes beyond any religious conventions and the Child of Light is not limited by any one belief system: "we do not name the Light-Bringer, but attune to the source that is *behind* the Names known to religion or cultural history." I think that's a deeply sensible approach, which works in relation to Brìghd as well. Beyond her role as a named saint and goddess, she is the fiery arrow which descends the Middle Pillar, guiding the spark of divinity into manifestation. As R.J. puts it:

> "The cosmic principle, the solar spiritual power, comes into a loving relationship with the ancestral goddess. This is part of the humanising process. It relates the Child of Light to ancestral consciousness, to the primal goddess of fire in action, and, specifically, to a location. That location is neither in the world of nature nor in the world of spirit: it is Avalon, which partakes of both. The Avalon location may be understood as Glastonbury, as in many folkloric tales and accumulated legends. This additional grounding of the imagery can be helpful, but it is not essential. ... The Avalon and Glastonbury referred to are not, of course, the current New Age tourist market of contemporary Glastonbury, but the deep spiritual, sacromagical and telluric foundation upon which all the many manifestations of Avalon and Glastonbury have developed through the centuries."[1]

So when we talk about Brìghd in Avalon, we may mean two separate but related things. We may mean the sacred site in

Glastonbury where Brìghd's powers are flowing and contactable. Or we may mean the inner Avalon in which Brìghd represents the ancestral matrix for these islands. Regardless of which we are concerned with, her powers are dynamic, fiery, inspiring and transformative.

Brìghd in Glastonbury

The legend has it that St Brigid of Kildare came over to visit Glastonbury in the early 6th century and founded a community of nuns in a place just south-west of the town, called Beckery.

It's hard to imagine now what this site would have looked like a millennium and a half ago when the area now known as the Somerset Levels was at best a heavy salt-marsh, and at worst fully flooded. Prehistoric wooden trackways have been excavated nearby which show how people used to have to traverse the area on raised planks. Instead of the sunken lanes which are found in so many parts of England, the ancient roads here were the opposite: raised causeways known as droves, with a drainage ditch either side, formerly used for transporting livestock. The landscape around Glastonbury is the product of centuries of human tinkering, largely through a network of drainage ditches known as rhynes (pronounced 'reens') which still have to be actively managed to minimise the risk of floods. In St Brigid's time, the pleasant green farmland around here would have been very wet and swampy or even submerged, with settlement only really practical on the higher ground of the hills and knolls. Bride's Mound at Beckery would have been an obvious choice for settlement.

Although it's only a very small hill, dwarfed by its neighbouring Glastonbury Tor, Beckery seems to have been in use for a very long time, with evidence of occupation going back to the Neolithic period. William of Malmesbury, writing in about 1129, mentions a 7th century Anglo-Saxon charter granting seven islands to Glastonbury Abbey by Cenwealh, King of Wessex. These were the Isles of Avalon, Beckery, Godney, Martinsea, Meare, Panborough and Nyland.

The island of Beckery comprises a low ridge rising to a small peak at its western end, delineated by the River Brue (which is not flowing in its original course here, but in an artificial channel made

The old church tower on top of Glastonbury Tor features a carved image of St Brigid milking a cow.

for the convenience of the Abbey). It's not clear how long the ridge has been called Bride's Mound; the name can't be traced back with certainty for more than a few centuries, but the fields here are traditionally known as 'the Brides' and there is a Bride's Mill marked on older maps. Inside this enclosure of fields, close by the River Brue, is the supposed site of Bride's Well, a sacred spring.

The legend of St Brigid was recorded by John of Glastonbury in about 1400, who claimed that she visited Glastonbury from Ireland in 488 A.D. and spent several years on 'Beokery' island, where there was a chapel dedicated to Mary Magdalene. The chapel was later re-dedicated to St. Brigid, either during her tenure or after it. It's been suggested that the name Beckery means 'Little Ireland', from the Gaelic *Becc-Eriu*, but this seems a bit tenuous and a more likely origin is the Old English *Beocere*. It's possible that Beckery chapel was used as a stopping off place for pilgrims on their way to Glastonbury Abbey. John of Glastonbury also makes mention of a 'monastery of holy virgins' on Wearyall Hill very close by.

Dion Fortune added her own contribution to the Beckery romance in her book *Glastonbury: Avalon of the Heart*, claiming that St Brigid "left her weaving-tools behind her, and a few years ago a bronze bell of most ancient workmanship was found there by a shepherd, and was given by him to Chalice Well ... That it was a woman's bell is certain, for the finger-holes by which it is held are so small that only a woman's fingers could use them."[2] It would appear that the whereabouts of the bell is no longer known.

Either way, the existence of an Anglo-Saxon monastic site was corroborated by an archaeological exploration in 1967, which

**The top of Bride's Mound at Beckery, looking west, with an
information board on the horizon.**

found the remains of three successive chapel buildings along with a
number of burials. The first timber or wattle and daub building was
either a chapel or a tomb-shrine, and seems to have been built over
a single burial in a cist. It has been dated to the late 8th century and
was replaced a while later by a stone building of late Saxon date. The
archaeologists concluded that there was "no evidence that there
was activity on the site in the 5th or 6th centuries, when according
to legend, the site was visited by St Brigid (c.450-523 A.D.), who
left some relics there."[3] The third chapel (plus a priest's house) was
built in the 13th century, completely enclosing the previous chapel
site, and was present until the dissolution of Glastonbury Abbey,
when it fell into ruin. Some of the ruins were still there at the end
of the 18th century but there's no trace visible on the surface today.
The accompanying cemetery was dated to the Saxon period and
contained 63 burials, all oriented west-east and interred simply,
with no coffin or fancy goods. Contrary to the tradition of female
occupation of this site, all except three of the burials were male.

Did St Brigid of Kildare come to Glastonbury?

I doubt it. Sorry, that's a very cynical answer isn't it? But what
with Jesus, Joseph of Arimathea, St Patrick, St Collen, St Brigid,
the Holy Grail, Lancelot and King Arthur, is there any important

figure or object in the Western Mysteries who wasn't trying to pile into Glastonbury to stamp their spiritual mark on it? Whether most of these illustrious visits, settlements and burials actually took place we will never know, and that's the simple truth of it. But as every Grail-seeker knows, the crucial thing is to ask the right question.

From a magician's point of view, it doesn't matter a jot whether St Brigid physically turned up and camped on a scrubby knoll above the Somerset marshes or not. It's not her one-time physical presence which forges the important connection, but her inner presence. The archaeological evidence may not back up the idea of a women's community at Beckery, but the legend of Brìghd has arisen for a reason and is not invalidated in any way by a lack of physical proof. *The powers of her office are functioning in that place*, as a magician might put it.

There are other legends whirling around the island of Beckery. One is that King Arthur had a recurring dream for three consecutive nights while staying at the nearby nunnery on Wearyall Hill, urging him to visit the chapel at Beckery. When he did so, he witnessed a vision of the Virgin Mary presenting the infant Jesus as the Blessed Sacrament on the altar. This has a striking similarity with the opening section of *Perlesvaus*, a magical Grail text which is credited with having originated "in the Isle of Avalon, at the head of the adventurous marshes". Again, is there any evidence to suggest King Arthur visited Beckery? Of course not, but if you use the site (either physically or in the imagination) to make contact with him, you are tapping into the established 'tracks in space' relating to the legend, the land and the archetypes, which may have powerful effects.

If what Dion Fortune said is to be taken at face value, and St Brigid's weaving tools were left at Beckery, then we have a similarly potent connection with the ancient British weaver goddess, who is another of Brìghd's ancestral forms.

Dr Goodchild and the Beckery resurgence

After years of quietly fading into the agricultural landscape, it's fair to say that Bride's Mound had a major spiritual resurgence in the early 1900s.

It could be said to have started at the close of the 19th century when John Goodchild, a spiritually-inclined English doctor working abroad in Italy, began to have psychic experiences relating to an antique blue glass bowl which he had recently purchased. He was told in no uncertain terms to take the bowl to Bride's Mound in Glastonbury and await further instructions. The opportunity took a while to come, but finally he got his chance to go and stay in Glastonbury for a few weeks, where he identified the relevant site using old maps. One morning he awoke early with a clear idea what to do; he took the antique cup to the place he had identified as the original site of Bride's Well, put it under the water and wedged it into a hollow underneath a stone.

The 'well' in which Dr Goodchild placed the cup was not the sacred spring itself, which no longer existed even in his day. It was actually a man-made sluice serving the system of drainage ditches, and may well have been little more than a muddy pond beside an aged and revered thorn tree. But he had done what was asked of him, and for several years afterwards it became a personal place of pilgrimage for him. In August 1904 he had the pleasure of escorting his friend William Sharp on a visit to Bride's Mound, an experience which made a powerful impression on both of them. It was on that occasion that William Sharp became the only person to whom Goodchild confided the story of the blue glass bowl. Interestingly, Dr Goodchild maintained a close written friendship for several years with both William Sharp and Fiona Macleod, having no idea that one was the channel of the other.

Goodchild had a keen interest – shared by Sharp – in what he called the "ancient Salmon of St Bride".[4] This took the form of a naturally sculpted effigy in the landscape, incorporating the site of Bride's Mound within the shape of a giant fish. He believed that local folklore sources backed this up. The site of Bride's Well (or the sluice which became its substitute) was in front of the salmon's nose and close to the River Brue.

Even at this time, however, Goodchild began to sense that the bowl was no longer there, and when he had an opportunity in 1905 to get into the sluice again and check, he did indeed find it was missing.

As he later learned, the bowl had been retrieved by Katharine "Kitty" Tudor Pole, a young woman whose brother, Wellesley, was an acquaintance of Goodchild's. The story goes that Wellesley Tudor Pole had had a psychic hunch and told his sister and a couple of other young ladies who were friends of the family that they should search in St Bride's Well during a forthcoming trip to Glastonbury. The full story can be found in Patrick Benham's book *The Avalonians*, but the upshot was that Kitty went alone to Beckery, waded into the mud and rummaged about until she found the blue glass bowl. She then went home to Clifton in Bristol and made an elaborate shrine for it, believing it to be an object of special sacred significance – even the cup of Christ himself. She and her friends established something along the lines of a magical religious order of St Bride, in which members of the public were invited to receive healing. Some of their beliefs and rites may appear a little romantic to us over a century later, but they were acting on a legitimate impulse. The bowl is now kept at Chalice Well.

Soon after, the indefatigable Alice Buckton helped establish a revival of interest in Bride's Mound as a spiritual site, initially with her pageant play *The Coming of Bride*. Then in the 1920s she created a Pilgrimage Route around the whole of Glastonbury which included a walk down Benedict Street and Porchestall Drove and onto Bride's Mound. En route, pilgrims were encouraged to tie clooties (votive rags) on a thorn tree near the site of Bride's Well, in the hope of attracting blessings or healing from St Brigid. By all accounts this practice was already well established: the clooties were in evidence during Goodchild and Sharp's visit in 1904, and were part of a long-held local reverence of this particular tree.

1   R.J. Stewart, *The Arch of Heaven* (R.J. Stewart Books, 2013)
2   Dion Fortune, *Glastonbury: Avalon of the Heart* (Weiser, 2000)
3   P. Rahtz and S. Hirst, *Beckery Chapel, Glastonbury 1967-8* (archaeological report, 1974)
4   Patrick Benham, *The Avalonians* (Gothic Image, 1993)

Originally published in Lyra 20, Lughnasadh 2015

First Thoughts on Esoteric Geology

W E live in a society in which magical interests are shunted off down one end of a polarised scale, with science and sensibility at the opposite end. Either you're a rational, hard-headed sceptic or you're wishy-washy, new-agey, credulous and gullible. One or the other! But this is entirely a false dichotomy. Science and magic are not polar opposites, they're just different ways of approaching the same realities; they are mutually reaffirming and compatible.

This wouldn't be news to the likes of Isaac Newton, who considered his work on alchemy to be just as important as his work on physics, and the fact that his alchemy writings have been brushed aside or even suppressed by an embarrassed scientific community who think they know better is a failing of theirs, not his. Overlaying magical material on top of scientific material, I usually find that not only do they line up, but they feed into one another and create useful and enlightening perspectives, opening up new avenues to explore. The only downside is that these perspectives can get very elaborate and complicated very quickly, opening up multiple lines of study and leaving you struggling to get your head round it all in a coherent way.

I don't have an answer to this. So this brief attempt to begin formulating a magical perspective on the science of geology should be seen as just that: scratching the surface of something that is very deep and could lead anywhere. Indeed I started out to write an article on *The Chemical Elements and the Lords of Form*, but this is what I ended up with! A greatly simplified focus on one small area of the topic I started out on.

In our magical endeavours we often work with the Planetary Being and align ourselves with the tides and cycles of Nature. For the most part we focus on cycles that we regularly witness in their entirety: seasons of the year, or the life, death and rebirth of creatures and plants. We don't focus so much on the cycles of rocks, even though they make up most of the substance of our planet and are there under our feet all the time. Indeed from our human perspective we tend to view rocks as symbols of stability, solidity and *non*-change. It is, however, just a matter of perspective, because rocks are in a continual cycle of change and rebirth which is every bit as dynamic as the turning seasons. It just escapes our notice because it's a cycle which plays out over millions of years!

We all know that the Earth is extremely old and that human life is a mere pimple on its anatomy. It's very hard to grasp the magnitude of this though, because our experience and intellect is too limited. It doesn't help us to say that the Earth is 4.54 billion years old because we can't imagine that, so we have to use an analogy, and I can't put it any better than the Open University science tutorial which likens the age of the Earth to a toilet roll, with humans representing just the last few perforations on the last sheet! This is a humbling concept to grasp, which is no doubt why so many 'young earthers' and Bible literalists still refuse to accept it. It's difficult to assert man's God-given dominion over the Earth when faced with the reality that we're barely a gnat's fart in the cosmic scheme of things.

However, we're here to make the best of what we are given. I've been thinking about the magical relevance of geology for a while, one impetus coming from a colleague who wrote about *feng shui* and explained how different energies can relate to different types of underlying bedrock. This got me thinking, because I'd long been aware how different parts of the country have a completely different vibe from one another, even when the countryside doesn't look that different. Could it be related to something as simple and unnoticeable as the underlying rocks?

Where I live in the Cotswolds, the landscape has a tremendously soft and comforting aura about it, which is one of the things that makes it such a nice place to be. The rock around here is a soft Middle Jurassic limestone with a golden honey colour, formed from layers of compressed sand and shells laid down on the bed of a tropical sea. At only 180 million years old, it's a relatively young rock. The faery presences here tend to be warm and friendly and very much connected to ephemeral expressions of nature, such as trees and springs. If I go a mere 20 miles up the road to the Malvern Hills I experience a complete change of atmosphere. The

Malverns feel like the ancient of ancients, and I'm aware of being in the presence of something incomprehensibly old; partly ancestral, partly something going beyond ancestors. The hills themselves are teeming with faery presences, but they're of a completely different order to the Cotswold ones: very old, very powerful, sometimes quite abstract, and very well established. You have to approach them with extra care and respect, as although they're not unfriendly they're not necessarily aligned with the concerns of humans. The Malverns are geologically ancient too, formed along a fault where the older Precambrian rocks have been thrust up to lie on top of the newer rocks. At 4000 million years old, the dense grey granites of the Malverns are among the oldest rocks on earth, formed when the planet was in the first flush of creation.

Going back to Essex where I spent my childhood, I always felt that the atmosphere there was a bit knobbly and I could never get quite comfortable with it; it's powerful enough in little pockets where you find faery presences very able and willing to work with humanity, but you have to search around for them or look a bit deeper under the surface. That pretty much sums up the geology of the area too, which is devoid of any surface rocks apart from alluvial deposits of pebbles, so it's all soil rather than stone – and you'd have to go some way down to find the underlying bedrock. Being mostly soil, the spiritual presences are often related to agriculture, and the only native stone you find on the surface are nodules of chert (flint): hard, bobbly lumps of quartz, which are very poor for building but brilliant for making practical tools.

The relationship between the geology of an area and the accompanying auras and presences is a lot more complex than these personal observations suggest, and numerous other factors come into it as well. For example, erosion of the limestone in the Cotswolds gives us an alkaline lime-rich soil, which supports a very different range of plant species from the Malverns with its acidic soil, and it's hardly surprising to find that different faery beings are associated with different expressions of the green world. Faeries who dwell among shady ferns are not the same as those found in the grassy wildflower meadows. And of course local rock also determines the choice of building stone – and thus the physical appearance of human settlements in the area – which also has an effect on the aura of a place. But we're not looking to get

bogged down in complexities. It's enough just to see that there is
a relationship between the inner life of a place and the underlying
geology.

But while we can muse freely on the things we feel in particular
places, and the ways we approach our inner plane contacts there, I
aim to go a bit deeper into understanding them. As with all things
magical, it's best approached through symbol and imagination
rather than by thinking about it too hard! So to help me grasp the
esoteric side of geology I've been using an alchemical emblem from
the *Musaeum Hermeticum* text of 1652 (shown opposite). This
image was pushed under my nose as soon as I started working on
the topic, and provides us with a wealth of useful symbolism.

The emblem shows three androgynous figures seated on top
of a mound holding symbol shields. Below their feet, the mound
is open to show seven shadowy figures sitting within its hollow
interior. At the very front is a well-shaft. The scene is encompassed
by a circular border and four corners containing planetary and
elemental symbolism.

The numbers 3 and 7 abound in alchemical emblems, but this
one is particularly relevant to the forces and forms involved in the
creation of rocks, and can be used as a key to the inner worlds of
geology. Of course that's not what the originator of the emblem
intended to convey: the science of geology didn't even exist in 1652.
But we're not seeking to explore the emblem in its original context,
which deals solely with alchemy and should only be interpreted
in alchemical terms. We're using it instead as a *magical image*, to
bounce our imagination off it for the purpose of opening up inner
worlds in a particular direction. This is a valid and powerful way to
use alchemical emblems, as long as we understand the difference
between the two approaches.

The original image is in black and white, but it's a very useful
magical exercise to print off an alchemical emblem, ideally onto
watercolour paper, and colour it in by hand. There is no shortage
of ready-coloured alchemical emblems on the internet which have
been done by others (Adam McLean is very good at these) but the
real learning experience comes from doing it yourself and there's
really no substitute for it. The beauty of it is that there's no right
or wrong way to colour these emblems, and you can use different
colour symbolism to create magical images for different purposes

or to emphasise different aspects. In this instance I made a hand-coloured version which emphasises the geological symbolism. I coloured the four elements at the corners with their traditional esoteric quarter colours while the main image in the middle used the colours of Malkuth: citrine, olive, russet and black, to demonstrate that the symbolism in this part of the image belongs to the realm of earthly expression.

Around the edges are the four elements in their traditional symbols, representing the archetypal elements throughout Creation. Between them is a sphere made from two crescents, each of which contains the seven planets and is a mirrored opposite of the other (to emphasise this, I coloured the 'below sun' silver and the 'below moon' gold, in opposition to what is above). They show us that the planetary influences are working in an above and below relationship, through the stars in the heavens and the stars within the earth.

The central image in the emblem is the group of three androgynous figures seated on a rocky mound, each with a tree behind them. These figures are forces of Nature acting within the realm of Earth, which in geological terms means Heat, Pressure, and Time/Space. They are the three driving forces for all that happens below. On their shields can be seen the upright triangle of Sedimentary rocks, the inverted triangle of Igneous rocks, and the combined triangles which represent Metamorphic rock and the creation of something different through the balance of the other two forces.

Below the mound are seven figures representing the crystal systems, or archetypal crystal forms. They also align with the seven planets and the seven planetary metals. Their forms are shadowy and normally hidden from sight, but we can see that the one in the centre is playing a lyre.

At the front of this scene is a well, representing an entrance to the realm of something else much deeper, in this instance the red hot iron at the core of the Earth. Note that although the well has a winch mechanism above it, there is no rope!

When I began delving into this topic, I started out by looking at some fairly pure and abstract esoteric concepts – the actions of the Lords of Form – and trying to apply them to an aspect of physical science, namely the periodic table of chemical elements. But I quickly found my focus becoming more narrow and specialised, and realised that I needed to consider the role of the Earth itself in all this – because the pure spiritual impulses of Lords of Form have to manifest through the processes of Earth, with all its great muddle of imperfections. I'm going to leave aside the chemical elements for the moment, because although they are extremely relevant and important, they also make things immensely complicated, and thus impractical to work with esoterically unless you focus on a small bit at a time. So for now I'm mostly going to forget about what the rocks are made of, and just look at the interplay of forces and forms which makes up their 'life cycle'.

We're all familiar with the idea that the Earth has a very hot interior consisting of magma, or molten rock, and that the surface is a relatively thin crust of separate 'plates' which move around and bump into each other periodically. The seemingly solid and inert ground beneath our feet is really whirling with dynamic change and flux, even if it's happening too slowly or too far down for us to be aware of it.

Contrary to popular belief, the very centre of the Earth is solid, not molten, with liquid magma flowing all around it. The heat in the centre of the Earth is a product of continuous nuclear reactions from the decay of unstable radioactive elements. A scary thought perhaps, but really an example of how the radioactive elements do serve an essential cosmic purpose, and are not just nasty dangerous things for humans to misuse. Without this ferocious nuclear furnace at the Earth's core, there would have been no creation of the landscape on the surface, and no ongoing cycle of regeneration and renewal.

Because the nuclear reactions within the Earth are ongoing, the core doesn't cool down. It's been blazing away down there ever since the planet was formed. But radioactive elements are not infinite; they create these intense temperatures by spitting out neutrons which gradually erode their atomic weight until they become different elements. Uranium, one of the radioactive elements in the core, will eventually spit out so much of its atomic nucleus that it turns into lead. Once it becomes lead, it is stable and doesn't decay any further. There is real food for thought here for alchemists; lead really is a fundamental base metal which represents a benchmark for atomic stability.

Although the core contains these radioactive elements, most of the Earth's centre is actually made of iron – which is also one of the most abundant elements in the Earth's crust. This too gives us food for thought, because iron another of the important magical metals and has centuries of folklore and superstition attached to it, often relating to its powers of protection or defence.

One of the most intriguing esoteric puzzles for me is the long-standing tradition that the Faery race abhors iron. This doesn't really make any sense, given the abundance of iron throughout the Earth's fabric and its importance in regulating the magnetic fields which protect the planet and enable life to thrive. How can faeries be averse to it when they're so closely associated with all things earthy? I suspect there is a riddle of some kind at play here, and the prohibition is not to be taken literally but as a signpost to something much more subtle.

So let's look at the creation of rocks. All rocks are made up of **crystalline minerals**. Minerals always have a fixed chemical composition and atomic structure, which gives them a very predictable geometry and determines the properties they express. The flint nodules of Essex are mostly made up of quartz, precipitated out of a silicon-rich liquid. Quartz is silica or silicon dioxide (SiO_2) and has a very sturdy, compact atomic structure which gives it its characteristic hardness. The limestone of the Cotswolds, made from the compressed shells of Jurassic sea creatures, is mostly calcium carbonate or calcite ($CaCO_3$) and is much more prone to change, because the carbon within it always wants to be reacting to make something else. Calcite is not usually very durable, and readily dissolves in acids, including rainwater, so it erodes and dissolves through the soil in a way that quartz doesn't. Exploring the properties of different minerals and the chemical elements which govern their volatility and colour is beyond the scope of this article, but it's a subject which does offer us a unique glimpse into a kind of Earth-alchemy, for those who want to take the time to study it.

What we are looking at for now though is a cosmic pattern of Threes and Sevens which occurs in the world of rocks and minerals, as shown in the alchemical emblem.

The Three Forces

From our magical point of view, there are three essential forces which come into play when rocks are formed. These are **heat**, **pressure** and **time/space**. Yes, I know time/space is two things and not obviously definable as a force, but in this context they are interchangeable and interrelated and serve a particular function, at least from an esoteric point of view. Heat can be seen as the primary, initiating force which controls transformation and movement. Pressure is the secondary, constricting, consolidating force which brings limitation and stasis. Time/space is an intermediary force which allows expansion into specific form, and applies pattern and order to the actions of the other two forces. (I'd like to be able to say that the three forces correspond to the supernal spheres on the Tree of Life, but they don't, really.)

Geologists classify all rocks into three types based on how they were made.

Igneous rocks are the products of the forces of fire. The most obvious and visible example is the rock formed by lava when a volcano erupts. Lava also spills out under the sea through fissures in the sea-bed. But igneous rocks also form unseen below the surface of the Earth.

Magma works its way up towards the surface by a simple process of conduction (i.e. heat rises). You can visualise it somewhat like a lava lamp, where the heat from below causes the blobs of wax to rise, only to cool gradually as they get further up so that they sink back down again. Some magma gets close enough to the surface that it cools completely and solidifies into a new rock formation. Correspondingly, some areas of existing rock get dragged down under the Earth by a process of subduction (the opposite process to conduction) where they are exposed to high temperatures, melt and become magma again. For obvious reasons, igneous rocks don't contain fossils; any remnants of life forms which find their way into the igneous process are simply melted down.

It would be wrong though to imagine that molten magma at the centre of the Earth comes all the way up to the surface to explode as a volcano. Most of the melting happens in small pockets or 'magma chambers' relatively close below the surface, and these have no direct link with the Earth's core. The reason for this is that the melting temperature of rock increases as pressure increases. Although the temperature of the Earth is much hotter further down, it's also subject to much greater pressure, which prevents most of it from melting. So the deeper regions of the Earth are relatively stable and balanced, despite the truly enormous forces of heat and pressure. It's only when you get near the surface that these forces express themselves in a more dynamic way when the balance between them reaches a tipping point and allows spontaneous melting to occur, producing the magma for volcanic activity.

So much for heat and pressure; the force of time/space is also important in the creation of igneous rocks, because it governs the formation of crystals.

Although the shape of crystals is determined by their chemical composition and atomic structure (which we'll look at in a moment), the actual manifestation of them is determined by the speed of cooling and, in some instances, the space available for them to expand into. In short, it takes time for crystals to form, and the slower the magma cools the larger the crystals in the resulting rock. A large blob of magma deep underground may take thousands of years to cool fully, resulting in a coarse-grained granite full of well developed crystals. A lava flow coming through a fissure near the surface may cool in just a few years, and produce a fine-grained basalt full of tiny microcrystals. At the extreme end of the scale, lava which is blasted out of a volcano into the open air cools so rapidly – within a few hours or days – that the crystals have no chance to form at all. The result then is volcanic glass.

Igneous rocks are therefore created by various combinations of the three forces, the main one being heat – but it should be remembered that the mineral content of magma (or rather, the chemical composition) determines the nature of what is formed. The minerals in their fiery molten state represent the principle of *potential*, while the three forces control how that potential is realised.

Sedimentary rocks are the second type and their manner of creation is completely different. If igneous rocks are formed by rapid change through the force of fire, sedimentary rocks are created by a process of slow recycling under the force of pressure, often over the course of millions of years. They are formed by the gradual deposition of small grains and particles into beds and layers. These grains might be from soils such as sand, silt and clay, remnants of organic life such as sea-shells, or fragments weathered away from older rocks. Over long periods of time these particles accumulate to quite a depth, and as the layers build up, the weight of the top layers presses down on the lower levels, squeezing out air and pushing the particles closer together. Gradually the sediments become so well compacted and cemented that the particles bond together into a solid mass and turn into stone.

It's not just virgin particles that make up this process. Much of the material comes from the breakdown of existing rocks through weathering. We are familiar enough with the effects of weathering and erosion in our environment, but we tend only to think about its relatively short term effects. Given a time period that runs into millions of years, even the largest and hardest of rocks are worn away by the ravages of sun, rain, frost, wind, heat and cold. This is going on around us all the time; the scree slopes on mountains are made from fragments ground away from the mountain itself, and the small pebbles on river beds are nature's tumblestones, worn smooth by being turned over and over. As these fragments are washed further away from their source by water, wind or gravity, so they wear down into smaller particles until they finally come to rest on sea beds and river deltas, to be compressed down into sedimentary rock. Creatures that live and die on the land or water may also be buried in this sediment and slowly lithified – sedimentary rock often contains fossils. Limestone, sandstone, chalk and shale are all examples of sedimentary rock.

Metamorphic rock is the third type and is made when existing rocks (either igneous or sedimentary) undergo changes and turn into something else. The metamorphic process often involves both heat and pressure in collaboration. Rocks may be heated up enough that they can be bent, folded, buckled and compressed, but without fully melting (if it does melt, it becomes magma, beginning the cycle all over again). Pressure may reach such extreme levels that certain chemical elements are literally squeezed out, changing the composition of the mineral. Metamorphosis is actually the way mountains are formed – layers of rock pushed together, buckled and forced on top of one another under immense pressure. The rock is also pushed down as well as up, and where it meets with the high temperatures deep inside the Earth it undergoes a partial melting, and more metamorphosis. Whether heat or pressure is the main factor involved, or both, the fabric and structure of the rock itself is changed, and it becomes something quite different from how it started. The cosmic principle involved here is transformation.

Gneiss is one of the best known of the metamorphic rocks, and the distinct folding and rippling patterns you see in the rock are the result of the metamorphic process. Many ancient monuments are built from gneiss, including the Callanish stones on the Isle of Lewis. Another well-known metamorphic rock is slate, which is made from shale (a sedimentary rock) which is compressed so densely that its molecular structure changes and it foliates (realigns into layers) so that it tends to cleave into flaky sheets. Metamorphic rock rarely contains fossils because of the destructive nature of the process, but where they do occur (e.g. in slate) they're often weirdly squashed and distorted.

These three forces combine to make a beautifully balanced cycle of renewal, a continual transformation of the rocks under our feet. Each stage of the cycle may take millions of years to complete, but it's going on all the time. The body of the Earth is in constant dynamic flux, despite the appearance, to our miniscule perspective, of being solid and unchanging.

The Seven Forms

Having looked at forces, we now turn our attention to forms: and in the world of rock that basically means crystals.

We're probably most used to thinking about crystals in terms of precious stones and gems, but the same principles apply to the minerals which make up the substance of rock, even if the crystals are less showy. What makes crystals special is their geometrically regular shape, which applies right down to their smallest component parts, their atoms and molecules. This geometric structure is a pattern or blueprint by which the formation of a crystal is predetermined – the shape of the crystal remains fundamentally the same regardless of what size it develops into.

I never cease to marvel at the near perfect cubes created naturally in pyrites and fluorites. If broken up, they tend to cleave along regular planes so that the smaller pieces are cube-shaped too. Ruby and sapphire in their natural form make beautiful regular hexagons. Quartz, of course, forms into six-sided columns with terminated points. Even sugar will crystallise naturally into tiny perfect cubes.

In practice you see a lot of diversity in crystal shapes, even in crystals of the same type. In the case of pyrites, for example, you don't just get perfect cubes but also higgledy-piggledy clusters of different shapes, and even 'sunbursts'. Fluorite occurs as octahedrons as well as cubes. But that's because their essential pattern is capable of expressing itself in a number of different ways. Even if they look quite different on the outside, their inner structure is regular and consistent. The key to understanding this is to look at the angles and axes rather than the shape *per se*. It's possible for a crystal's faces to take on a number of different shapes *but the angle between them remains constant.*

The atoms and molecules which make up a crystalline substance are arranged in spatially precise geometric patterns, with no wasted space, in perfect order. These patterns are known as crystal lattices, and their geometry is confined to one of seven shapes: square, hexagon, triangle, rectangle, rhombus, parallelogram and trapezium. **Crystal systems** is the name given to the variety of forms created by each shape. So for all the diversity in the Earth's rocks (and ones in other parts of space for that matter), the number of different patterns of crystal geometry is only seven.

The magical number seven brings us back to our alchemical emblem. The seven figures sitting in the cave under the mound were most likely intended to have a planetary significance, lining up with the row of sun, moon and stars which appears above and below in the emblem. But those seven planetary figures can be extended to the geometric attributes of the seven crystal systems, opening up a whole new line of esoteric potential. They can also be extended to the symbolism of the seven planetary metals, which are another whole area of study and meditation in their own right. Let me emphasise again that *we are not looking at what the originator of the emblem intended to convey in his image*, which is purely concerned with alchemy. We are looking to project the emblem onto a new set of symbols as a magical image, and use it as a key to another door.

The table on the next page shows how the symbolism between the crystal systems and the planets and 'seven metals' archetypes might line up. These are my own tentative attributions and they may or may not be the best ones to use. Please feel free to rearrange them however you choose, if you are following up on this work. As with most systems of magical correspondences, there are no absolute rights or wrongs, it's just a case of finding something that works.

When we talk about the planetary metals it's important to distinguish these *archetypal* metals from the actual physical metals found in the Earth and its rocks. Metals do generally have a crystalline structure but unfortunately it's not a simple case of matching them up neatly with the seven crystal systems. Copper, silver, gold, iron and lead are all cubic, while tin is tetragonal and

Crystal system	Shape	Planet	Metal	Rock-forming minerals include	Gemstone crystals include
Cubic	▢	Sun	Gold ☉	galena, halite (salt), magnetite, copper, silver, iron, gold	fluorite, pyrite, diamond, garnet, lapis lazuli, sodalite
Tetragonal	▯	Mercury	Mercury ☿	cassiterite, chalcopyrite, scapolite	apophyllite, zircon
Hexagonal	⬡	Jupiter	Tin ♃	pyromorphite, vanadinite	beryl, aquamarine, emerald, apatite, sugilite, morganite
Trigonal	△	Venus	Copper ♀	oolite, rhyolite, calcite, granite, dolomite, marble, haematite	ruby, sapphire, quartz, tourmaline, rhodochrosite, tiger iron, dioptase
Orthorhombic	◇	Mars	Iron ♂	sulphur, olivine, marcasite, barite, zoisite, cerussite	topaz, prehnite, danburite, iolite, chrysoberyl, tanzanite
Monoclinic	▱	Saturn	Lead ♄	hornblende, muscovite, gypsum, biotite, diopside	malachite, chaorite, moonstone, chrysocolla, lepidolite
Triclinic	▱	Moon	Silver ☽	porphyrite	larimar, amazonite, labradorite, sunstone, rhodonite, turquoise

mercury has no crystal structure at all while in its liquid form at ambient temperature! So the metals listed here apply to the planetary and alchemical context only.

Those who like to work with crystal healing might find it interesting to see whether the inner geometry of the crystal has a bearing on its healing properties. Many crystal healing books place an emphasis on the colours of crystals, choosing them according to which chakra they influence. But my feeling is that this might be just one of many factors worth taking into account. The colour of a rock or gem can be very variable but its inner geometry is consistent right down to the atomic level.

Squaring the circle

Having put our rocks and minerals into seven tidy categories, we still have some that are unaccounted for. The seven crystal systems are the only geometric shapes possible, but what about those which don't actually have any geometric shape? Crystal formation requires time, and as we saw in the section on igneous rocks, if molten rock is cooled rapidly it has no chance to form any crystals whatsoever. This includes obsidian (volcanic glass) and moldavite (spatters from an ancient meteorite). Others may only have a crystal structure in certain conditions, such as mercury which has none while it's liquid. In other cases, crystals fail to form because too many different things are blended together, as with amber and opal. We could look upon this group as a separate, eighth crystal system called 'amorphous'.

When we take our seven crystal systems with their eighth or zero non-system and compare them with the layout of the periodic table of chemical elements, we have another interesting similarity. The periodic table comprises seven groups of elements plus an eighth group which doesn't behave the same way. This is the group of noble or inert gases, which are atomically balanced and therefore don't react with anything, and are traditionally numbered zero. And so we're back where we started, given that it was the periodic table which set me on this quest to discover the magic of geology!

Sources and suggested reading:
Gienger, Michael *Crystal Power, Crystal Healing* (Blandford, 1998)

Park, Graham *Introducing Geology, 2nd edition* (Dunedin, 2010)
Stewart, R.J. *The Sphere of Art* (R.J. Stewart Books, 2008)
McLean, Adam *Study Course on Alchemical Symbolism* (privately published, 2011)

Originally published in Lyra 22, Imbolc 2016

Anthony Duncan and the Challenge of the Extraterrestrial

I NEVER actually met my dad's close friend the Reverend Canon Anthony Duncan. He was curate at Tewkesbury Abbey in 1964 when he baptised my elder brother, but had moved on to another parish in the Forest of Dean by the time I came along in 1969 (I had the pleasure of being baptised by the Rev. Cosmo Pouncey instead). A few years later he moved again to the first of a series of parishes in Northumberland, and so I only got to know him through the long letters he would write to us at Christmas, and the cards featuring the

superb landscape photography of his son Iain. His presence in the background of my life was always strong through his ongoing friendship with my parents, and I was very sad when he died suddenly in 2003. Several years later I found myself in a position to reissue some of his books which had fallen out of print, and it has felt like an important service to do so.

Around 2011 Tony's widow, Helga, paid a visit to my parents with a box of unpublished manuscripts. Nobody had really been through them since Tony's passing to see what was in there, so the pleasure of discovering these new and unseen scripts fell to my dad. Among the treasures contained in the box was a spine-tingling unpublished novel, appropriately called *Unfinished Business*, which was closely based on Tony's experience of living in the haunted rectory at Parkend in the Forest of Dean. There was also a pair of manuscripts called *The Liberation of the Imagination* and *To Think Without Fear: The Challenge of the Extra-Terrestrial*. Both of these were discussions of the possibility – or even likelihood – of extraterrestrial contact. Also in the box was a personal memoir, printed in the pale grey type of an old Amstrad dot-matrix word-processor, making it abundantly clear that Tony's views on alien visitations were based firmly on personal experience.

Well, 'challenge' was the operative word. I knew all about Tony's extraordinary natural psychic ability, and his encyclopaedic understanding of ghosts and hauntings in all their diverse forms, which had led the Church of England to commission him to write a short guidebook on the psychic disturbance of places for private use by the clergy. I knew that he was also highly familiar with the realm of Faery, and that his ability to see and perceive them led him to accept and respect them as part of God's Creation – a controversial and brave position for a C of E vicar to take. But aliens? That was a new one on me.

The manuscripts duly arrived on my desk, since my dad felt they were important works and well worth publishing. It was thrilling to leaf through these documents and be among the first to read them. They eventually saw the light of day in 2015 as a single volume called *To Think Without Fear*. But even as I worked through the editorial process, I wasn't quite sure what to make of it all. The idea of extraterrestrials turning up at a Northumbrian vicarage seemed a bit far-fetched somehow. But why? After all, I have no trouble believing in faeries! I see faeries everywhere when I'm out on my country walks, along with ancestral presences, elementals and assorted other beings which aren't on most people's radars, and I take the existence of such things for granted. Perhaps it's the non-earthly aspect of aliens which makes them harder to get my head round? But no, I've have had plenty of dealings with star beings of one kind or another in my esoteric work, not to mention the angelic hierarchies!

I came to realise eventually that the problem was me – and that I'd allowed myself to slip into that mindset I'd always prided myself on *not* being subject to, namely the Closed Mind. It's not that I don't believe in extraterrestrials. On the contrary, given what we know about the size of the universe, it would be far-fetched indeed to suggest that Earth is the only planet which hosts life. But I'd settled into a comfortable little esoteric worldview in which Faery was normal, Archangels were welcomed, ghosts were an occasional sideshow and I didn't have to think about a lot else.

The difference of course is that most of the contacts we work with in our esoteric practices are non-physical, and rarely make tangible incursions into the physical world. When they do, it tends to be in small symbolic ways. But I assumed that aliens share the same physical reality as us. In which case, the prospect of UFOs as alien spacecraft seems highly implausible, simply on the basis that they are unlikely to be exempt from the laws of physics. There are few potentially inhabitable planets within 1000 light years of us, so unless we want to tear up Einstein's most famous theory we have to accept that it would take an alien spacecraft 1000 years to get here if it was travelling at the speed of light, which is in itself a bit of a stretch, as it's unlikely that any living thing could survive travel at such speed.

There's also the question of why; however pompous our sense of our own importance, our planet is in a sparse backwater of an insignificant galaxy. Why would anybody even find us? It's not easy to have a sensible discussion of what such a contact might be like either, as our ideas about aliens are poisoned by the hostile and destructive stereotypes of popular culture. For me this was epitomised by the 2002 film *Signs*, in which crop circles are discovered to be guiding signs for the invasion of Earth by 7ft-tall three-clawed monsters, who mercifully can be fended off by whacking them in the goolies with a baseball bat. Such is the puerile level of human imagination on this subject.

But the reason Tony Duncan's contact with extraterrestrials was such a challenge to me in my cosy esoteric world was that it had nothing to do with UFOs or the bulbous-headed freaks of popular imagination. It came instead as a mind-to-mind psychic contact. Yes, the same way we esoteric types communicate with faeries, ancestors, deities and whatever else we work with. For some reason, this possibility had never before crossed my mind. If extraterrestrials are not reliant on physical presence or physically-transmitted messages, and can communicate directly to those who are psychically receptive, then suddenly an entire universe of possibilities is opened up.

Far from being sinister or threatening, the Duncans' visitors were exceptional in their politeness. The following is an extract from Tony's personal account:

2nd December 1995

Some two or three years ago we became aware of being "visited" in some way, usually at night, by persons who we came to understand as alien to our own Earth and humanity. They were not visible but their presence was sensed psychically.

Following upon one such visitation, at night, Helga had occasion to visit the bathroom, and both on her way there and on her way back, she became aware of a soft but unmistakable hum, as of an electrical transformer, coming from just outside the house, in or very close to the stable yard. Nothing was visible but something was unmistakably "there."

Within the last week or so this phenomenon has reoccurred at our new address. I woke up, suddenly and with total wakefulness, to a strong sense of "presence." At the same time I became aware of a soft but unmistakable humming sound, coming – as it seemed – from the bay window of the bedroom. It was as if the unseen source of the sound was half in and half out of the room.

After a few moments the sound altered as if its source had increased power and "lifted off." The sound became steadily more distant and then ceased. At the same time I became aware that the sense of "presence" had also ceased.

One or two evenings later – it may have been the next day – we were reading and watching TV in the drawing-room. We both heard the dining-room door, behind the dividing curtain between the rooms, twice give a sound as if something was pushing upon it. The door is inclined to stick and sometimes releases tensions caused by pressure during the closing of it and so we did not take too much notice at the time.

A little later, however, something caused me to investigate, and on opening the door into the hall, I was confronted both with an almost overpowering sense of "presence" and a great sense of tension. This was evidently a Visitation of some consequence.

I said "Peace be with you!" and, in prayer, was told who they were and what I must do. I greeted them in the Name of our Lord and of the Holy Trinity, I welcomed them and accepted them and said that, whatever the Will of God for us both was, I would work with them. I say "them" because there seemed to be a group present rather than an individual.

There was an immediate relaxation of tension. I realised that they had been quite apprehensive as to my reaction to them. We were now, quite evidently, friends. I returned to watching TV and told Helga all about it. She was not particularly surprised.

A half-hour or so later there was a loud knock on the dining-room door. I opened it and encountered the "presences" again. I was puzzled by this and sought, in prayer, an indication of what I should do. I was told that they were waiting to be invited to depart! Good manners! I greeted them again and bade them farewell for the time being. The "presences" then faded from my consciousness.

I was given to understand that they belong to the same Universe as we do, that they might be described as humanoid but are better understood as Elementals of their own place than as Human in the way we are on Earth. I was given to understand that clairvoyant vision would have seen them clearly (I am very seldom clairvoyant) and that they may well become visible to me in due course and that their appearance would occasion me no alarm if they did!

This seems to be a "gateway" exercise as far as I am concerned and I await developments. I make no speculation as to the cause or nature of the electric-sounding hum.

Over a period of some years, it seems, Tony and Helga and one of their grown-up sons encountered these non-terrestrial visitors on such a frequent basis that they became known simply as "our chums". The initial encounter was with a small group of two or three unseen presences who turned up in the kitchen and larder of the vicarage at Whitley Mill, and at night in the bedroom. When the Duncans moved to a new house in Corbridge the visits resumed within three weeks, suggesting very plainly that such contacts are made with people and not places.

Gradually Tony identified four distinct and separate groups of visitors, who were not only of different origin but perhaps not even aware of one another. One of these groups he described as "tall, solemn beings whom we were given to understand belonged to a different universe altogether", although communication with these was limited due to their remote nature. Another group was found to be more invasive and less highly evolved, and these were politely and kindly banished.

But the majority of the contacts came from a group of highly developed individuals, perceived to be about 6 feet tall, with whom a genuine rapport of mutual affection and respect was quickly established. Visits by this group were welcomed (once it had been impressed upon them that sleep was a necessity of human life and they should not therefore turn up in the middle of the night) and Tony began to experiment with taking written communication from one of them, whom he affectionately named "Jimmy". During this period he also devoted a lot of time and thought to the implications of these contacts.

I became persuaded that my new acquaintances were alien. They were "foreign!" But they were peaceful, even friendly. Who were they?

There is much speculation about visitants from "Outer Space" and there is an abundance of literature describing encounters with "flying saucers" and unidentified flying objects of many descriptions. There are accounts of encounters with humanoid beings, apparently from such craft, and even of abductions of men and women for short periods and of their detailed examination by their abductors. There is also every sign of obsessional silence and "security" by officialdom on this matter.

Let me say at once that I have no difficulty in accepting the possibility – even the probability – of there being a substantial body of truth in all this. The various "explanations" of these things are a great deal less credible than the acceptance of their essential possibility. I keep an open mind.

Were my visitants the crew of an Unidentified Flying Object? Was a Flying Saucer parked, cunningly concealed, close to the Vicarage?

I have no hesitation in dismissing any such idea. Why? An inner awareness that this is so.

Not only an inner awareness, however. The Flying Saucer type of phenomenon has to do with *a technology*. Supposing that there is a hard core of truth and reality at the midst of the "U.F.O and Alien" controversy, we appear to be encountered with beings not too unlike ourselves who are dependent upon technology in order to visit us. We are impressed by a technology we cannot yet understand.

What does this technology achieve? Does it fly from, let us say, Venus or Mars, at unimaginable speeds? Or does it, by some means, *change wavelength* and come from another, and quite invisible, environment into our own, and back again?

We don't know and it may be some time – supposing these reports to be factual – before we do know. But, however "advanced" this might seem to be, it remains very much at our level. It is a technologically-enabled intrusion, benevolent or otherwise. It is effected *from without*, it is not from within.

We project our own problems upon others and we project our own hostilities and insecurities upon everything strange or alien. Our mental images of inter-planetary travel are demonised by our obsession with "Star Wars." Being children of Adam and Eve, we take it for granted that Cain will always kill Abel. Our first instinct (faithfully manifested in our fictional literature) is to call in the military!

I am quite persuaded that my Foreign Friends were – indeed are – peaceful, benevolent and anxious to be friends. I did not project "Star Wars" upon them, nor they on me. There was, however, a slight tension in our mutual awareness until I held my arm out to them and said "Peace be with you!" At once the tension vanished, and its release was mutual.

I am also persuaded that their entry into our consciousness was not dependent upon external hardware of any description. The "technology" was interior, if such words can be used. A bridging continuum between one set of coordinates and another was established and there was a meeting, possibly less of minds than of hearts.

Remembering the definition of prayer as "standing before God with the mind in the heart," the proper basis for any meeting of minds must be, in any event, between minds-in-hearts.

Inevitably, a large part of Tony's thought was devoted to how these experiences could be reconciled with the Christian faith. Believing the alien contacts to be fellow denizens of Creation, on the same basis that Faeries are part of Creation, is the easy bit. But where does Christ fit in? Redemption through the Incarnation is taken by the Church as cosmic, universal and eternal. Do the extraterrestrial visitors have any knowledge of, or need for, the Christian mystery? In conversation with the contact "Jimmy", the message was received that they have no awareness or experience of it, but are fully respectful.

Tony did come to the view, however, that his visitors were essentially human, but *differently evolved*. He suggested (speculatively of course) that mankind's current lot, apparently alone in a vast, lifeless and meaningless universe, is part and parcel of our banishment from the Garden of Eden, which may not have been an Earthly realm at all. That we ourselves could be the ones who are 'alienated' by way of our lumbering physicality, obliged to live effectively as animals, stuck in a closed-off and frequently self-destructive condition of mind. Meanwhile our extraterrestrial brethren are fellow humans who have been through their own lengthy evolution by trial and error, but separately from us, and are occupying the same universe (or universes) on a different "wavelength" which we cannot observe from the very limited standpoint of our mortal life-state, but which may be closer than we realise.

But why now? And what do they want? There's no question that the number and frequency of reported extraterrestrial encounters has been on the increase during the last few decades. At face value this feeds the sceptical view that most people are just imagining (or lying about) such experiences, given that there didn't seem to be much of it before mankind's own adventures into space travel and exploration caught the popular imagination.

Perhaps the visitations have been going on for longer than we realise but humanity needed to expand its imagination before comprehension of them was possible. Or perhaps, as Tony was inclined to think, there may be something about the Earth's Aura which, for an unspecified period, rendered it impenetrable – perhaps even invisible – and which is only now "thinning out" sufficiently to make visitation possible.

As he put it: "A convergence is in progress and both human and humanoid are part of it." That would certainly chime with those who believe that 2012 heralded a global consciousness shift which is currently in process.

As for their intentions, Tony Duncan was in little doubt about that. "There is neither malice nor malign intent in any of our Extra-Terrestrial visitors. They are not to be perceived as a threat to us in any way. They come, almost entirely, to look, to meet, to greet and to befriend."

Originally published in Lyra 25, Samhain 2016

Anthony Duncan's book *To Think Without Fear* **is published by Skylight Press**

The Magical Constance of π
or, why the circle is a sacred symbol

IF there's one magical symbol which can lay claim to be fundamental and universal, it has to be the circle. The 'magic circle' has been used to delineate a magical working space for as long as anyone can remember. In the practice of ritual magic in the Dion Fortune and Gareth Knight tradition, we begin and end almost every working with three circumambulations of the Lodge, which can be seen as representing the three Rings of Space in *The Cosmic Doctrine*, a sophisticated way of defining a temple space in modern magical practice. The ancient art of 'casting the circle' uses the circle for much the same purpose – that of defining and delineating the temple. Since time immemorial, magicians of every stripe have laid out their sacred space by scratching a circle into the earth.

But why a circle? Why not a square or a rectangle? Of course some sacred spaces, such as churches, do take the form of a rectangle, and this has its own magical symbolism which will have to wait for another article. But the circle is the default. King Arthur's Table Round was chosen because the circular shape enabled the entire fellowship to sit around it as equals. But while that aspect is important, it's not the whole story. The circle is an inherently sacred symbol, so fundamental that it holds the first key to Creation. In order to understand its deeper significance, we have to take a closer look at pi (π), the mathematical constant which is the relationship between the diameter (width) of a circle and its outer perimeter. Every study of circles – and spheres – comes back to pi.

Let's start off by dredging up memories of school maths lessons and reminding ourselves what pi actually is. If only our school teachers had taken a more esoteric viewpoint then the whole thing might have been a lot more interesting.

Pi is a transcendental number beginning 3.14159 but which potentially goes on forever. It's usually represented by the Greek letter π, pronounced 'pie', although pedants may enjoy the Greek pronunciation 'pee'. The use of the symbol only goes back three hundred years; it was first applied by the Welsh mathematician William Jones in 1706, and it's thought that he chose it because it's the first letter of the Greek word for 'perimeter'. However, pi itself has been known about for millennia and many of the finest minds of the past few thousand years have been devoted to trying to define it. Although the first accurate formula for calculating it was devised in 14th century India, there's evidence to suggest that pi was known and understood in a more basic form by the ancient Egyptian pyramid builders, ancient Chinese geometers, and very possibly the ancient Britons, including the builders of Stonehenge. Anyone, in short, who was in the business of constructing circular monuments.

Pi is the ratio between the diameter of a circle and its circumference. It is a mathematical constant, but defining its exact value is an impossible task: it cannot be represented as a fraction, and when put into decimal form it has no end. Modern computing has allowed us to calculate π to trillions of decimal places but no complete value for it can be reached and no pattern or repeating sequence has been found. It just keeps on spitting out seemingly random digits into eternity.

The circle's status as a sacred symbol is held in simplest terms within this ratio, $1:\pi$. A circle inherently contains a relationship between the known and the unknowable, between the finite and the infinite, between the fixed and the transcendent. It doesn't matter what size circle it is or what unit of measure is used, this ratio relationship remains constant. This is no idle fact to occupy a moment's curiosity, it is a profound glimpse into the mechanics of the Universe. The circle, in effect, has its being in two different realities and as such is a gateway between the fixed world of matter and the realm of the inscrutable and eternal.

A unique property which the circle/sphere has, which is not shared by any other geometric shape, is the constance of the relationship between its centre and its perimeter (i.e. the radius). Any given point on the circumference is the same distance away from the centre as any other point. This is the reason why a compass is used for drawing circles; the radius is the fixed distance between its two arms. Place one arm of the compass onto your central point and the other will describe a circle no matter which way you move it. If you need to map out a circle without a compass, you can push a stake into the centre point and stretch out a string or rope to measure the distance out to the circumference. This will create a perfect circle as long as the rope's length is kept constant. No point on a circle's circumference can ever be any closer or further away from the centre than any other – otherwise it's no longer a circle.

It follows that every circle needs to have a centre and a radius in order to exist, and that these give rise to the third element: the circumference. Now we are getting into the realms of Qabalah!

We can look upon the three elements of the circle as a representation of the three Sephiroth in the Supernal Triad.

Kether represents the centre of a circle, which exists in a balanced state of simultaneous being and unbeing; where the potentiality of everything is held in a perfected equilibrium with nothingness. A circle's centre is undefinable and infinite, in the sense that it has no dimensions and can be reduced to a vanishingly small point which, like π, can remain constant while expanding to infinity.

The circle's radius/diameter is an expression of **Chockmah**. It's the first movement into creation, the pushing out of Kether's stillness into something defined and tangible. It creates and defines a space between the centre and its outward expression. In doing so, it creates the first spatial dimensions.

The circumference of the circle is **Binah**, a delineation of the limit and boundary of the first stable form, space with a perimeter around it. It constricts the expansion of the radius while being the direct product of it. A new state of dynamic balance is formed, and the rest of Creation flows out from these three initial principles. The circle is the universe's firstborn.

This principle was not lost on William Blake, whose engraving *The Ancient of Days* shows the Creator within a circle emerging out of radiant light and reaching down through a veil of grey cloud to stretch out his compasses across the surface of the Void.

The Barbury Castle Pi

One of the symbols I've found compelling to meditate on in my pursuit of circle magic is a formation which appeared in a field of barley on 1st June 2008 near the hillfort of Barbury Castle in Wiltshire. Crop circles remain a matter of controversy and ridicule;

William Blake's 'The Ancient of Days', engraved for the frontispiece of 'Europe, A Prophecy' in 1794. It shows Urizen as the Divine Geometer, emerging from the veil or cloud of mystery to outline the proportions of Creation by setting the axes of his compasses across the Void. Although he is shown in human form, his domain is the Cosmic Circle behind which shines the Limitless Light of Ain Soph Aur. In drawing the first circle of Creation he defines its limits and brings it to order. In doing so he creates the first ratio, between the diameter he has drawn and the undefinable transcendence of π.

they were very fashionable around 1990 and have since dropped out of public consciousness to such an extent that many people don't even realise that they're still appearing, year after year, often in the same fields, in increasingly complex patterns. Where they come from – who designs them and who makes them – I genuinely have no idea, and I won't bother to speculate. There are two things I can say with some confidence though. One is that most are not made by jokers with ropes and boards. The other is that whoever is behind them has a spectacular understanding of esoteric geometry.

It pays to rise above the debate about their origin and simply take them at face value. They are a visual medium, and the most immediate way to engage with them is just to look at them.

There are many striking images which have appeared as crop circles, but very often the most significant aspects of their geometric construction is implied or hidden, and reveals itself only when you spend a bit of time studying them visually (or better still, drawing them). The Barbury Castle formation of 2008 takes the form of a weirdly erratic stepped spiral inside a circular frame, plus a few smaller dots and blobs. It took a few days before anybody noticed that the stepped spiral fitted to a set of invisible guidelines which become obvious when you draw it out on paper.

By dividing the circle pizza-like into ten equal slices, and also into ten equal concentric rings, the pattern reveals itself. Starting in the centre and following the line of the spiral, you can count along three slices before meeting with a small circular 'point', after which the spiral arc jumps to the next concentric ring. Only one slice is covered by this arc of the spiral before it jumps out to the next concentric ring, where it traces four slices and jumps out again, then one slice, then five slices, then nine... If you follow this pattern of counting all the way to the end, taking the small dot near the middle to be a decimal point, then the spiral spells out 3.141592654 – in other words, π! (True π is 3.141592653... so the last digit has been rounded up.) The spiral ends at a row of three circles of diminishing size which can be seen to represent the ellipsis.

The Barbury Castle Pi is an exquisitely clever and elegant way of expressing π in circular graphic form. It manages to combine radial geometry and concentric geometry in one neat glyph, encapsulating the dynamic polarity between the feminine force which turns the circle and the masculine force which expands the

circle outwards. Studying it further will reveal additional elements of hidden seven-fold, nine-fold and ten-fold geometry, while also resolving the ancient conundrum of 'squaring the circle', symbolic of the harmonisation of the Divine (the circle) with the Material World (the square). As a meditation symbol, this crop circle design is a gift, wherever it comes from.

True pi and 'fudge' pi: the magical sum of 22/7

Way back before π was a thing, ancient peoples understood that circles have this inherent contradiction between the defined and the undefinable, not least because it impacted the practical task of calculating the proportions of round buildings. If the true value of π is an infinite number which cannot be measured, then a fudged version has to do for practical purposes. There are various options for simplifying π into something workable, but the most common one, favoured by many cultures from the Ancient Greeks onward but possibly also used in Ancient Egypt, is the value 22/7. In other words, if a circle's diameter measures 7 (in units of whatever), its circumference measures 22. Dividing 22 by 7 gives you 3.1428, which is not quite π but it's accurate to two decimal places, and for most practical purposes that's good enough. To put it in perspective, if you built a circular wall a mile in circumference using 22/7 rather than true π, then at the end of it your measurements would be out by a mere 2ft. For practical circle-building, the margin of error is fairly negligible.

What is striking for any student of the Qabalah and other esoteric systems is that the sum 22/7 is in itself a magical one. It relates most obviously to the Hebrew alphabet, which has 22 letters, of which there are 7 'double letters' which have a dual nature and thus a certain symbolic affinity with the circle and its inherent being in two worlds at once. There are also of course the 22 paths on the Tree of Life, and 22 tarot archetypes in the major arcana, while the number 7 is familiar to us in the number of traditional planets and alchemical metals, amongst other things.

The conclusion to draw from this is that π is a magical concept whether it's used in its perfect transcendental form or in a slightly compromised practical adaptation. It's designed to function in the imperfect world of material form as well as in the realm of the Divine.

A circle is a state of equilibrium between the Created and the Uncreate, a simple and perfect union between manifestation and eternity. It is the first geometric shape and the first form inscribed by the Divine Geometer. As such it forms a space where the Divine is ever present. The key to its temple is π.

Originally published in Lyra 26, Imbolc 2017

The Severn Bore

NATURE has her way sometimes of making humans feel very small and completely at the mercy of her magic. Who hasn't felt that humbling awe on witnessing a lightning storm or a fierce gale? But one of the more graceful and understated displays of her power is the bore wave which can be witnessed along a stretch of the River Severn between Sharpness and Gloucester. The Severn Bore is a tidal surge, a large wave which goes the wrong way up the river during certain tidal conditions. Its timing is very regular and its ultimate mistress is the Moon.

I began my life just a few yards away from the River Severn in Tewkesbury, where the frequent flooding sometimes left us cut off from the rest of the town in our lonely house on the hill. I grew up with the common misapprehension that the Severn Bore was a once-a-year event, but it isn't. It occurs on around 130 days a year, with a wave forming at each turning of the tide, which makes for 260 bores a year, although they vary in size and impressiveness. The peak times occur in the days just after the Full Moon and the New Moon, with the biggest waves usually forming around the Spring and Autumn Equinox. Because it's a product of the tides, its occurrence and timing can be predicted with reasonable accuracy, give or take about 20 minutes to allow for localised variations in the weather.

The tidal wave is initially formed way out in the ocean and gathers in height as it's funnelled up the Bristol Channel. This is only enabled by the particular shape and geology of the Severn channel – which is why you don't get bores on most rivers.

In places where the river is wider and deeper, it can be seen only as a roll on the surface. But as it surges upstream and the channel narrows, it's forced into a peak which moves against the natural flow of the river at a speed of between 8 and 13mph, pushing its way upstream as far inland as Gloucester – or even further if it's high enough to overcome the weirs in its path. The surging wave is spectacular when it's at its best, but even more startling is the rapid and massive rise in the water level which follows in its wake.

The Severn is not a kindly and friendly river at the best of times. Unlike the velvety green River Avon nearby, it's a cold, steely grey river whose inscrutable surface hides many dangerous currents which have claimed numerous lives since time immemorial, and still do. One tiny church near the river still has its antique wheeled bier built for the purpose of retrieving the (often unidentified) corpses which were fished out of the water on a regular basis. In its entirety the Severn is a massive 220 miles long, rising from a spring at Plynlimon in the Cambrian Mountains of Wales and taking a circuitous route down to Somerset where it becomes the Bristol Channel and merges into the seascape which laps around Brean Down, the home of Dion Fortune's Sea Priestess. One of its striking features as it flows through Gloucestershire is a large horseshoe-shaped bend which was a sacred place to our Roman and Celtic ancestors, and which when viewed from any vantage point on the hills on either side appears as a great silver torc snaking across the landscape.

The remains of several Celtic temples have been found in the region of the horseshoe bend, including a major Romano-Celtic temple at Lydney dedicated to a local god known as Nodens. It has been speculated that Nodens could be specifically a god of the Severn Bore, as the tidal waves must have inspired awe in our ancestors as much as they do today. The Romans also worshipped a goddess of the River Severn called Sabrina, who was almost certainly adapted from an earlier local goddess whose precise name is forgotten. That the river and its bore were given divine status is no surprise to me at all, because the magical energy generated by the bore wave and its aftermath is really something which has to be experienced to be appreciated.

The first time I saw the bore was in August 2013, when it produced one of its larger waves. It came late in the evening when it was already dark. I stood on the bank at Minsterworth on the western side of the river with a bright full moon shining on the water, which was still and glossy before the bore arrived, like black glass. I didn't see the wave coming – I heard it! Its approach was heralded by a loud rushing noise like an approaching train. Then the black water just heaved up – forming into a huge smooth wall of water which dashed the moon's reflection into tiny turbulent shards. It was amazing, beautiful, humbling and more than a little

The night-time Severn Bore passes through Minsterworth under a full moon, 22nd August 2013, rippling with reflected moonlight.

scary. What I hadn't been prepared for though was the aftermath, because the most magical effect comes after the wave has passed by. Not only was the rushing black water churning about like a choppy sea and lapping the top of the bank, it was actually running backwards – flowing upstream, and at some speed. It was carrying large items of debris – a whole tree-trunk was whooshed upstream as if it was a piece of driftwood.

The river continued to run backwards for well over an hour after the wave had passed, and for all that time I couldn't take my eyes off it and couldn't walk away. There was a strong lunar energy being generated, not least because of the beauty of the full moon reflecting in the water, but largely because this whole phenomenon is a direct product of the moon's power – and she wants you to know it.

I finally got to see a daytime bore in April 2017, and although it was a smaller and quite modest wave, its magical energies were no less impressive. This time I was standing on the apex of the horseshoe bend at Arlingham on the eastern side, looking across to the west bank and the small town of Newnham on Severn. There used to be a ferry crossing here which ran for centuries, up until the

Surfers ride a small bore wave below the town of Newnham on Severn on 29th April 2017. Within a few minutes of taking this photo the sandflats were completely consumed by a churning mass of water.

end of the Second World War, but now it's long gone and the river is uncrossable at this point.

I stood here looking across towards Newnham, so close and so unreachable, over a large expanse of sand. And then it came – that same rushing roar like an express train. The wave itself was much smaller than the previous one I'd witnessed (which didn't stop a handful of surfers from having a go on it) but the sense of raw elemental power was mind-blowing, and once again I found my tears welling up at the sheer sense of magic it brought with it.

As the wave disappeared round the corner the rushing sound grew louder and the water level began to rise rapidly – very rapidly. It took barely five minutes for the vast sandflats to completely vanish under a tide of churning, turbulent brown water which looked more like a raging sea than a river. It came right up to the top of the bank where I was standing and I soon had waves breaking at my feet.

But the physical spectacle was only half the story, and once again I was struck by the dynamic energy surging and churning all around me. It was completely mesmerising and I stood and basked in it for the best part of an hour. During that time, as before, the river ran backwards.

When the churning waves had finally eased it was like a normal river again, but still going the wrong way. Logs, branches, barrels – everything was flowing *up*stream with power and purpose.

There is nothing else quite like the Severn Bore; it is unique. I doubt I will ever tire of seeing it – it humbles and alarms me but leaves me energised and empowered. If you want a truly mind-blowing display of the power of the Moon, just watch her drag the Bristol Channel into a tidal wave and heave it all the way up to Gloucester. It's not something you'll ever forget.

Originally published in Lyra 27, Beltane 2017

The Nine Herbs Charm

IN the British Library is a beautifully hand-written Anglo-Saxon book dating back to the late 10th or early 11th century, known today as the *Lacnunga* (Remedies) although the original has no title. It's a compendium of recipes, remedies, collected herbals, prayers, invocations and spells, mostly written in Old English. The Nine Herbs Charm is one of its best known excerpts and gives us a startlingly direct and detailed example of English magical practice 1000 years ago.

On the downside, although an invocation to the herbs and some practical instructions for the ritual are given, it's not always clear exactly what was meant! The text is vague and muddled in places. Translating it into modern English is not straightforward either, as some Old English words are ambiguous or fell out of usage so long ago they've been forgotten, so that we can only now guess at what

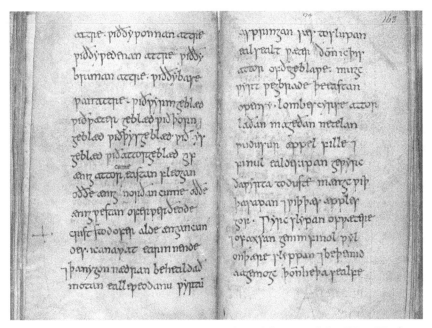

Folio 162-63 of the Lacnunga manuscript with part of the Nine Herbs Charm (British Library, Harley MS 585)

the original meaning was. In some cases the meaning can be very different depending on how you choose to interpret certain words. There is, I suppose, a touch of irony that we don't have any way of accurately understanding a text when it's written in English.

Unfortunately the parts lost in translation include the names of some of the actual herbs. The charm does include some descriptive details about them, but not all of it is helpful and although scholars and botanists have all applied their brains to it, there's no consensus on the identification of some of the herbs. This would seem to make the charm impossible to perform, or even to fully understand. Not that this has stopped people from offering herb blends for sale on the internet, purporting to be the authentic recipe.

It's not even certain exactly where the charm begins and ends, as it's sandwiched between other remedies in a continuous text, and it veers from herbal invocation to magical ritual to recipe instructions with no obvious break. Given that the *Lacnunga* is made up of collected material it's possible that the charm has been drawn together from different sources and become garbled. We don't really know whether it's meant to be the way it is or not!

The Nine Herbs Charm is certainly quite an unusual piece among surviving Anglo-Saxon texts. Much of the *Lacnunga* consists of recipes for herbal remedies of the don't-try-this-at-home variety, ranging from the sensible, e.g. horehound for lung disorders, to the downright dodgy (burst skin eruptions, anybody? Slap on some hot ox dung!)

At face value, the charm's purpose appears to be for healing an infected wound. It eulogises each herb for its powers in standing against poison and infection, before making an invocation asking the herbs to banish poisons of every kind. It then has an extraordinary magical interlude in which Woden is described using 'nine glory-twigs' to strike against an adder. There then follows a more conventional herbal remedy section explaining (sort of) how to prepare the herbs and apply them to the patient. There is more ritual content here too, as it specifies that the charm should be sung over each of the herbs and also into the ears and mouth of the patient.

Clearly we aren't in a position where we would want to try to perform the charm as written. It has every appearance of being a healing spell, but in truth, we can't know what its exact purpose

The Nine Herbs Charm
(translated into modern English)

Remember, Mugwort, what you made known,
What you established at the Great Council.
Unique, you are called, the oldest of herbs.
You have power against three and against thirty
you have power against poison and against infection,
you have power against the loathsome one roving through the land.
And you, Plantain, mother of herbs,
Open from the east, powerful within.
over you chariots rolled, over you queens rode,
over you brides cried out, over you bulls snorted.
You withstood and confronted them all.
May you likewise withstand poison and infection
and the loathsome one roving through the land.
'Stune' (lamb's cress) is the name of this herb, it grows on stone,
it stands up against poison, combats pain.
'Resolute' (nettle) it is called, it attacks against poison,
it drives out the hostile one, it casts out poison.
This is the herb that fought against the serpent,
it has power against poison, it has power against infection,
it has power against the loathsome one roving through the land.
Put to flight now, Poison-loather, as lesser the greater,
as greater the lesser, until he is cured of both.
Remember, Chamomile, what you made known,
what you accomplished at Alderford,
that never should anyone lose their life from infection
once Chamomile had been prepared for their food.
This is the herb that is called 'Wergulu'.
A seal sent it across the sea's horizon,
a vexation to poison, a remedy to others.
It stands against pain, it fights against poison.
A worm came crawling, it bit a person.
Then Woden took nine glory-twigs,
and struck the adder so that it flew apart into nine pieces.
There Apple accomplished against poison
so that it would never re-enter the house.

Chervil and Fennel, twosome of great power,
They were created by the wise Lord,
holy in the heavens as he was hanging;
He set them and sent them into the seven worlds,
for rich and poor, as a help to all.
It stands against pain, it fights against poison,
it avails against three and against thirty,
against foe's hand and against powerful scheming,
against enchantment by malevolent creatures.
Now these nine herbs have power against nine super-spirits,
against nine poisons and against nine infections:
Against the red poison, against the foul poison,
against the white poison, against the pale blue poison,
against the yellow poison, against the green poison,
against the black poison, against the blue poison,
against the brown poison, against the crimson poison,
against worm-blast, against water-blast,
against thorn-blast, against thistle-blast,
against ice-blast, against poison-blast,
if any poison comes flying from the east,
or any from the north comes,
or any from the west, upon the people.
Christ stood over diseases of every kind.
I alone know of a running stream;
there the nine adders keep guard.
May all the weeds spring up as healing herbs,
the seas part, all salt water,
when I blow this poison from you.
Mugwort, plantain that is open at the east, lamb's cress, poison-
loather, chamomile, nettle, crab-apple, chervil and fennel, old
salve; pound the herbs to a powder, mix them with the salve and
the juice of the apple. Then prepare a paste of water and of ashes;
take the fennel, boil it in the paste and anoint with a beaten egg
when you apply the salve, before or after.
Sing the charm three times over each of the herbs before
preparing them, and likewise on the apple. And sing the same
charm into the mouth of the man and into both his ears, and over
the wound, before applying the salve.

or context would've been, at this remove of time. We also have to remember that the Anglo-Saxons were people, just like the rest of us. The natural tendency is to glorify the past, but we can't assume that their magical practice was flawless any more than ours is (imagine if in 1000 years' time there was one surviving esoteric book – or new age spirituality book – from which people had to reconstruct all our beliefs and practices. Horrible thought, isn't it?) When dealing with the magical legacy of the Saxons or any other past civilisation we must remember to honour them but not idolise them.

The benefit in studying the charm is in what it provides to us in the way of Anglo-Saxon magical lore. This applies to both inner and outer. Our challenge from the inner point of view is to use it as a doorway through which we can make our own contact with the ancestral beings behind the Old English tradition. My experience is that the Anglo-Saxon contacts are very much present and active on the inner planes and they very much want to be seen and worked with.

Let's look first at the herbal content of the charm. Herbal medicine was a major part of Anglo-Saxon life, and was known as leechcraft. This is derived from the word *læce*, meaning doctor, and has nothing to do with leeches. The term 'wort' which is commonly seen today as a suffix on plant names is a modern spelling of the Old English *wyrt* (pronounced the same) and gives us a good indication of which plants were regarded as healing herbs by our forebears. Examples include St. John's wort, which has had a resurgence in recent years for treating depression (I can personally vouch for it), and woundwort, which was formerly used, well, for treating wounds. The way in which the herbs are addressed and appealed to in the Nine Herbs Charm suggests that they were regarded as sentient spiritual beings, and not just physical plants. Something akin to what we would now call a plant oversoul.

The nine herbs, with their Old English names, are as follows:

Mucᵹwyrt – Mugwort

This is a very common roadside weed which we all probably pass every day without noticing its attractively feathered leaves. Not quite so attractive is its taste, which is extremely bitter. Mugwort comes into its own as a magical herb rather than an ingested one. It has long been associated with travel – presumably because of its habit of growing at the sides of roads – and also as a herb of protection. Therefore it was traditionally carried as an amulet for protection while travelling in the hope of a safe journey.

It can be considered sacred to the goddess Artemis, whose name is enshrined in its botanical name, *Artemisia*, and to Diana. Its traditional medicinal uses include a wide variety of disorders specific to women. Mugwort also has a long and potent track record as a shamanic herb. Used dried, it can be stuffed into a 'dream pillow' to place under your head while sleeping, or burned as an incense before scrying sessions to enhance visionary experiences, and for prophecy and divination. There's more to this than simple folklore, because mugwort has mild psychoactive properties, and the smoke from its incense may well have an effect on your inner vision!

Ưeybrade – Plantain

The Saxon name means 'waybroad' and has been identified as plantain, partly based on the description in the charm which indicates a plant growing on waysides and trackways which can survive extensive trampling underfoot, but also because plantain appears under the name waybroad in other herbals from later periods. Its medicinal use includes the healing of insect bites, cuts and wounds, and it's supposed to have anti-inflammatory and anti-bacterial properties, which would make it a good herb to include in a charm against infection.

Stune or lombes Cyrse – unknown

Despite it being mentioned twice in the Nine Herbs Charm under two different names, we're none the wiser as to what it refers to. The name *lombes cyrse* translates into modern English as lamb's cress (not curse!) but it's not clear what that might be. One possible candidate is the plant known as lamb's lettuce or cornsalad. Under its other name, *stune*, the herb is described as a plant which grows on stone. There is no obvious answer to the identification.

Stiðe or Netelan – Nettle

Also appearing under two different names in the charm, nettle is easily identified here. The name *stiðe* or *stithe* (the letter ð is no longer in our alphabet but its sound is 'th') means strongly or harshly. The power of nettles to bring health and healing as well as its familiar sting is well known in the modern age, and it's still popular as a herbal tea or cordial. In fact it's something of a superfood – very nutritious and full of vitamins and iron, and surprisingly it tastes pretty good as well. It has associations with strength and fortitude, because its sting makes it a plant not-to-be-messed-with, while anyone who has ever tried to dig up its yellow web-like roots from the garden will understand its qualities of tenacity.

Attorlaðe – Betony or Nightshade?

The Old English word *attorlathe* means 'poison-loather'. That doesn't narrow it down a lot, which leaves the identification largely down to guesswork. One of the proposed candidates is betony, a wonderful healing herb and native English wildflower, but in a later section of the *Lacnunga* there are recipes which list both betony and attorlathe as separate ingredients, which would seem to undermine this interpretation. There is an intriguing tradition that serpents would fight and kill each other if placed within a ring of betony, which resonates with the symbolism of the Nine Herbs Charm, and also a superstition that wild animals would seek out betony to heal themselves if they were wounded. There are traditions for its magical use as well, as a protection against malevolent magic. It was grown extensively in monastery herb gardens for use on a variety of ills.

It has also been suggested that *attorlathe* could be cockspur grass. I'm not sure on what basis that identification has been made.

The most viable alternative candidate is black nightshade. Other herbals from the post-Saxon era give *attorlathe* as an alternative name for black nightshade, and certainly it's a potent shamanic herb, if one which needs to be treated with great respect. Nightshade is a common native British plant and although it's very poisonous, it has a number of traditional medicinal and magical uses. It might seem strange for a poisonous plant to go by the name of 'poison-loather', but it has a traditional use as a healer of abscesses and skin infections, as well as an internal use for cramps and spasms (don't try this at home).

Mæyðe – Mayweed or Chamomile

There are many different types of chamomile growing wild in England, all with different properties, and it isn't clear which one is referred to here. The one commonly known as scented mayweed is a strong candidate. Chamomile has a long history of medicinal use and is still popular as a soothing, calming herbal tea. The description in the Nine Herbs Charm refers to *maeythe* being used at a place called Alorford or Alderford. What this refers to, while it might have been common knowledge to the Anglo-Saxon reader 1000 years ago, is now a mystery.

Wergulu or Wuðusuræppel – Crab apple

Bitter-tasting tiny apples are an age-old feature of the English hedgerow, and I'm sure many of us have made the mistake of trying to eat one at some stage in our childhood. Mercifully for anyone on the receiving end of the Nine Herbs Charm, its pulp is specified for use as a salve, to be applied externally, with the other herbs mixed into it. The Old English name *wudursuræppel* usually translates to 'wood-apple' or 'wild apple'. As a remedy, crab apple is very cleansing and purifying. There is a long tradition of making cider from crab apples, for medicinal as well as recreational use, but it's not known for sure whether the Anglo-Saxons did so or not.

Fille – Chervil or possibly Cow parsley

This herb is thought to translate as chervil, although it's not a native herb in Britain. It was probably cultivated in monastery herb gardens though. It's also possible that it refers to the common native weed of the meadows, cow parsley, which is sometimes known as wild chervil, but we don't know for sure. As well as being a culinary herb, chervil has a traditional magical use in helping to attune your awareness of your inner immortal spark and to see beyond the immediacy of your present life.

Finule – Fennel

Another non-native herb, but one which was nevertheless grown and used by our Saxon ancestors. It has a long history of medicinal use and is good for aiding digestion, and for freshening the breath (try chewing one or two seeds, if you can take the strong aniseed flavour, and see how refreshing it is). It's very aromatic and was traditionally used as a pesticide, especially against fleas.

From an esoteric practitioner's point of view, the interesting thing is not so much the identity of the individual herbs as the manner in which they're used, invoking the inner powers of the herbs as much as the outer.

There is a 'banishing' of the poison from the quarters which would not look out of place in a modern magical ritual today. It is interesting that the banishing is done to the East, North and West, but not the South. I have a tentative theory that Anglo-Saxon rituals were run from the South, rather than the East as we traditionally do in modern magic. The practitioner using the charm would be standing in the South to do the invocation, hence the need to banish only in the other three directions.

Having called upon the powers of the herbs, it swiftly moves on to the god Woden.

The Saxons didn't go in for large pantheons of gods the way other cultures did, but they had a select band of deities, of whom Woden is by far the most important. He is the ancestor-god of the English. They considered him to be the root and origin of the English race, a father-god and guide and protector, and a bringer of wisdom and learning. He is of course closely related to the Norse god Odin, but the English had their own way of looking at things and the Woden contact is quite distinct from Odin.

Woden, in my experience, is a very stable, consistent and reliable contact who keeps everything on an even keel. The traditional image of him is rather daunting, as a grim old man with an eye missing. I don't think this is the whole story. His grim outer appearance serves as something of a Dweller on the Threshold of the Mysteries to deter those who lack understanding or respect. A more enlightened way of looking at him is to regard his 'lost' eye as being open on the inner rather than the outer. With one eye permanently alive to the inner worlds, he becomes an all-seeing visionary god who is well placed to dispense wisdom.

The fact that Woden and Christ are both called upon within the Nine Herbs Charm has been met with much head-scratching from scholars and lay-people alike. It seems to be a contradiction, doesn't it? Or perhaps an indication that the original pagan charm has been meddled with by prissy monks? Actually, no. The more time I spend with Anglo-Saxon material on both inner and outer, the more sure I am that our ancestors would not have seen anything strange or conflicting about this. The casting of Christian and Pagan as incompatible rival religions is a relatively modern one. It wasn't until very late in the Saxon period that disapproval was expressed towards pagan things and before that, it would've seemed very natural for the new religion to be happily incorporated into the old.

There are many examples of this in surviving Saxon texts. In this particular charm, Christ is described as standing against all kinds of disease, while Woden is a worker of practical healing magic. They both serve a similar role, except that Christ oversees the healing on a higher arc while Woden attends to the task in hand. There is also a curiously ambiguous section which refers to two herbs being created by the Lord as he was hanging in the heavens. This may be a reference to Christ, but it could just as easily refer to Woden who brought the magic of the runes through into the world after hanging for nine nights on the World Tree (a yew tree for the Saxons, in contrast to the ash tree of Norse legend).

Woden's association with runes may give us a clue as to what the 'nine glory-twigs' are. We can refer once again to the arrangement of nine staves (see page 58) which is commonly known as the Web of Wyrd. The Saxon concept of Wyrd is not dissimilar to the concept of karma, and indeed this glyph is a kind of Tree of Life which can be seen to encompass all things, an entire Universe through space and time, seen as a net of interconnected threads. The 33 or so runes of the Anglo-Saxon Futhorc can all be fitted within the geometry of this ninefold grid. Although there's no specific mention of runes in the Nine Herbs Charm it would make a lot of sense for the 'glory-twigs' to be either rune sticks or the nine staves of the Web of Wyrd.

It's probably fair to assume that the adder, serpent or 'worm' (take your pick of ways to translate the Old English *wyrm*) refers to a spiritual principle or an innerworld being, and not to a physical snake. It's often interpreted as a spiritual manifestation of the poison or infection, and that may be so, but I wouldn't want to jump to any conclusion about that, because we can sometimes lose sight of the meaning if we take things too literally. It is curious that Woden strikes the adder with the nine sticks and it then flies into nine parts. Again there are ambiguities of translation, but I'm inclined to see the nine parts of the adder as vital components of the healing, rather than it just being about destroying a malevolent being. It is as if he is activating the charm in some way by striking the adder. Given the importance of the magical number nine, it seems significant that these nine parts are created, and that they serve a definite magical purpose.

Sources:
Stephen Pollington, *Leechcraft: Early English Charms, Plantlore and Healing* (Anglo-Saxon Books, 2000)
The English Companions Members Handbook (privately published, 1998)
Bill Griffiths, *Aspects of Anglo-Saxon Magic* (Anglo-Saxon Books, 1996)
Paul Beyerl, *The Master Book of Herbalism* (Phoenix Publishing, 1984)

Originally published in Lyra 40, Lughnasadh 2020

Leylines and Coathangers
My life as a Dowser

O F all the 'minority interest' hobbies which helped shape my esoteric worldview, one of the most enduring is also one of the ones I talk least about. Dowsing is an art which doesn't have many practical applications in the work of a ritual magic fraternity, so it tends to sit on the sidelines as an activity for the weekend, whose insights only occasionally have relevance to esoteric matters. But it is a part of who I am, and was actually one of the first psychic activities I got into.

When I was a kid I avidly read occult books, which is not surprising given my background, even if it did cause occasional consternation at school. From an early age I would seek out every book I could find about ghosts, magic and psychic powers. It was in one of these, in 1979, that I first read about dowsing and followed the instructions for how to cut up a couple of wire coathangers and use them to locate the water pipes in the back garden. It worked, but it didn't take me long to get bored with it (well, I was 10) and I lost the rods. I didn't think much about them again until the prospect of dowsing piqued my interest for a second time at age 17, and I thought "I wonder what happened to those coathanger rods I made years ago?" I opened my wardrobe door and they came tumbling out at my feet with a clatter. It remains one of the weirdest unforgettable things that's happened to me. I'd been using that wardrobe on a daily basis for seven years without seeing them.

By this time I had developed a passionate interest in ancient sites, and it coincided with my having an older boyfriend who shared the same interests and had a car, so we used to go on regular trips to Avebury. On one of these visits I bought a copy of *Needles of Stone* by Tom Graves from the Henge shop, a book which was a life-changing read for me. To this day I'm not sure whether I can get my head round all of it, but it introduced me to something that became a lifelong fascination: the subtle lines and spirals of energy which course over, under and through the landscape.

According to the book these lines, invisible to the eye and unacknowledged by conventional wisdom, come in a startling diversity. They form straight lines, parallel lines, random meanders, spirals and knots. Some are below ground and some are above ground and in multiple 'bands' at different heights. Some attach themselves to 'node points' such as standing stones and church buttresses. Most have a polarity or 'charge' of some kind. They can be static or they can have a direction of flow or a direction of spin. Some appear to be related to underground water, or to electrical discharges. Some have an effect on people living near them and can even be responsible for hauntings. They can be found at most ancient sacred sites but also in a lot of other places, aligning with roads, tracks, hills, earthworks, springs and other features. The book also made the case that ancient monuments were a means by which earth energies could be directed and managed, not just by our ancestors but in the present day, with many links and alignments between sites – leylines – across the landscape. The author was a dowser who wrote compellingly about energy lines from the standpoint of practical understanding, because he could actually detect them. With a couple of bent coathangers.

Naturally having found this revelatory book at age 17 I had to go straight out and find some leylines, which is when my dowsing rods obligingly fell out of the cupboard. First of all I learned my craft with mundane stuff – getting my brother to flush the bog so that I could dowse for the water gushing down the sewer pipe under the garden path. For me, the angle-rods (held one in each hand) swing together and cross whenever I go over water or negatively-charged energy. They open outwards when I cross any kind of threshold or boundary, or over positively-charged energy. Once I'd got this basic skill, finding earth energies in the real world was not difficult. One of the things that I learned from *Needles of Stone* was that pre-Reformation churches almost invariably have underground water lines (or negatively-charged earth energy lines) running through them, entering and exiting the building in alignment with one of the windows or doors. What's more, there is usually a knot of two or more water lines, often called a 'blind spring', directly under the altar. This had to be tested!

Armed with my bent coathangers I went to a medieval church in a nearby village, and nobody was about so I snuck into the chancel and tried it. When I moved the coathangers over the altar, they crossed. They also reacted at various other points which appeared to line up with the architectural features of the church. It was a wonderful discovery and 30 years later I still find exactly the same patterns, in different variants, whenever I dowse inside a church. Most old churches seem to sit on top of a leyline, often running straight up the middle from the west door to the east window. I've rarely come across a church which doesn't have a knot or a crossing point of water lines under the altar, and that includes ruined churches and the sites of altars which aren't there any more.

This immediately raises a question: were churches purposely built on existing energy lines, or are the energy lines somehow created by the presence of the church? I'm afraid it's a question which I can't even begin to answer. It's the dowser's great conundrum and people have been falling out over it since the 1930s. All I can say is that I've found the phenomenon to be real enough from a dowser's point of view.

And what's true of churches is also true of barrows, standing stones, henges and just about every other kind of ancient monument in the landscape. They thrum with subtle energy. Many of us in the field of ritual magic are well aware of these energies, whether we're dowsers or not. But what dowsing is useful for is detecting the finer details.

Tom Graves was one of the dowsers involved in the Dragon Project in 1973, studying the nature of earth energies, and spent some time dowsing the Rollright stones in Oxfordshire. He noted that all the stones in the circle had their own energy 'charge' which changed or flipped polarity on its own individual cycle, sometimes over a few days or a few hours, while some had changes occurring every 20 seconds. He also discovered that the Rollright circle has concentric rings of alternating polarities from the centre outwards. In other words, if you walk in a straight line from one side of the circle to the other, your coathanger angle-rods will alternately cross over and open out, swinging first one way and then the other, as you walk across the circle. According to Graves there are seven concentric rings inside the stone circle and at least another three extending outside the stones, and possibly beyond. I've dowsed the Rollright circle many times and he's absolutely right. In fact it's become my Rollright party piece whenever I visit the site.

Before I go any further I should say that there is confusion around the term 'leyline', which is commonly, but often wrongly, used to describe earth energy lines. Properly speaking, a ley line is a simple alignment of visible features in the landscape, as described in *The Old Straight Track* by Alfred Watkins, who coined the term. These don't in themselves have anything to do with earth energy, although it's not uncommon for earth energy lines to follow them. Watkins was concerned only with alignments of physical features, and so some people prefer to use the term 'energy leys' to differentiate the earth energy lines from mundane ones. But among many dowsers and earth energy buffs the term 'leyline' with its misappropriated meaning has stuck, and we have to live with it.

As I went through my teens I did a lot of dowsing and much experimenting. One of the more interesting experiments I did with my brother involved dowsable thought-forms. One of us would create a ball of light in the air, the size of a football, using visualisation and the focused power of our thoughts, and the other would then come into the room and try to dowse for it. It worked almost every time. I introduced several people to the art of dowsing, as it really is a skill which almost anybody can pick up, even if they don't believe in it, and it is very gratifying to see the look on the face of a sceptic when the rods move in their hands without them doing anything. I reached a level of ability where I could dowse without rods – I could simply hold my hand out and feel the dowsing responses as tingles in my fingers. I can't really do that any more, but it was very handy for those occasions when I wanted to dowse more discreetly.

In the late 1980s I bought a rather pricey plastic V-rod from the British Society of Dowsers and couldn't get on with it at all to start with, but then one day something clicked and it's been my favourite tool ever since. I still use the same one. It's basically made from two lengths of springy material bound together at one end, and is a modern version of the traditional forked 'hazel switch' used by water diviners since time immemorial. It's really just a matter of convenience, because a traditional hazel twig has a short shelf life and really needs to be cut fresh from the hedgerow every time. The method is to bend the two arms of the rod in opposite directions while gently pushing them together. It takes a little while to get the hang of it, but the trick is to balance it so that it's held in a state of unstable equilibrium. From this neutral position the rod can

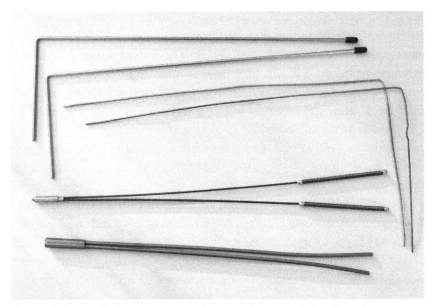

Tools of the trade. From top: modern angle rods with safety tips; my original home-made coathanger angle rods from 1979; a swanky new metal V-rod from the British Society of Dowsers and (bottom) my old plastic V-rod bought from the Society in the 1980s.

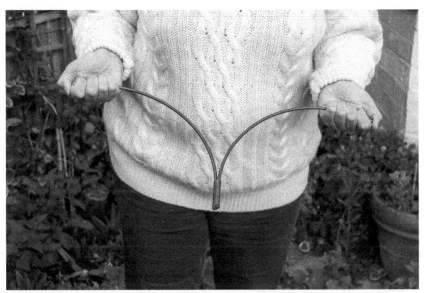

The V-rod in use. V-rods are based on the traditional dowser's forked stick and work in exactly the same way. The handles are bent opposite ways and pushed together, creating an unstable tension which can then flip the rod up or down.

easily flip itself either upwards or downwards. For me, upwards is for positively charged energy and boundary lines, downward is for negatively charged energy and water. The V-rod is not a versatile instrument because it can only do a simple up or down, but that's why I like it – it's decisive and unambiguous. And yet it's not without subtlety: I often feel it gently tugging and twitching in my hands as I approach a dowsable line or object, and it can be sensitive to the most delicate field of influence. Yet when it wants to react decisively there's no stopping it – I've had the friction marks on my hands to prove it.

Dowsing tools are not limited to the traditional by any means. The legendary dowser Hamish Miller, who discovered the Michael and Mary lines, used to dowse with a single angle-rod. Some people invent their own. My time in the British Society of Dowsers in the late 1980s brought me into contact with some very innovative and beautifully eccentric people. I remember going on a field trip to Hailes Abbey with the Worcester Dowsers and seeing somebody dowsing with a personal stereo. He was walking around with headphones on staring at the little machine and I asked him why. He told me that if you tune the radio to white noise with a mono signal, and walk around with it, the stereo light comes on whenever you walk over an energy line. I've no idea how that worked, but I watched him doing it and sure enough the small red LED on the radio came on in all the same places that my dowsing rods had reacted. Another lovely man in the group had designed and built his own dowsing machine, a strange and unwieldy contraption which he wheeled along on the end of a long handle, the wheel having been taken from his daughter's bicycle – with or without her permission I didn't like to ask.

There is, of course, a problem which haunts every dowser of 'earth energies', and which is not such an issue for water diviners: the problem of verification. For the traditional water dowser it's relatively straightforward: either the water is there or it isn't. You can dig a hole and find out. But with earth energies you have no way of knowing whether your results have any objective reality or not. I don't know what it is I'm picking up with my rods half the time, I only know that I'm picking up *something*. I call it 'earth energy' for want of a better name and assign it an arbitrary polarity, but I can't be certain whether it exists, let alone why it's there and what it's doing. The problem is compounded because different dowsers don't always get identical results – leading to not unreasonable criticisms that dowsers only pick up what they expect to find. There is no simple answer to this: dowsing responses are filtered in the mind in the same way that psychic communications are, so everyone experiences slightly different things. Complete objectivity is not possible, and self-delusion is all too easy. I can only advocate being as honest as possible in the dowsing process and keeping constant vigilance against lazy expectations. I think the reason that different dowsers find different things is often down to the complexity of what is being dowsed for, and the tendency of every dowser, consciously or otherwise, to attune themselves to a particular range of responses. Consciously attuning the mind to the exact thing you're dowsing for is a necessary and normal practice to filter out clutter, but it can mean that you tune out things which other people tune into. I think that the best you can aim for is to get results which are consistent. Regardless of whether you're in tune with other dowsers, you need to be in tune with yourself!

Needles of Stone Revisited, by Tom Graves, was published by Gothic Image in 1986.

Originally published in Lyra 27, Lughnasadh 2017

Index